T0288916

A SOLITARY TRAVELER
IN THE LONG NIGHT

A SOLITARY TRAVELER
IN THE LONG NIGHT

Tong Jun
The Later Years 1963–1983

Written by Zhang Qin
Translated by Howard Goldblatt

images
Publishing

"We meet the world, and yet transcend it, which is to say, we employ the brilliance of ideals to understand the undifferentiated nature of sadness and joy, and impassively observe the waves of humanity's glory and ignominy from the vantage point of an ideal realm."

Wang Guowei[1]

— CONTENTS —

— PREFACE —

Artists are expected to work with and through material media. However, when circumstances pose limitations and the world deals unfairness and trials, their resolve rises to the occasion: they work with their own lives. In doing so, they produce great artworks, using their own lives as the medium. Such was the story of Tong Jun (1900–1983). Born with a lineage of Manchu nobility, he grew up with memories of a vanished world and trying circumstances of a tumultuous time: the fall of the imperial Qing dynasty, and the subsequent decades when the nation was looking for its identity and new directions. His architectural training in the University of Pennsylvania (UPenn) in the U.S. and his extensive travels in Europe made him a citizen of the world—a self-identity that he held onto until his last days. His exquisite and sensitive watercolors register his impressions of his itinerary perceptions of Europe and the civilizational memories of human achievements.

When he returned to China, he was determined, and destined, to materialize and map that perception of civilizational grandeur onto a clean slate of the future of his native land. But reality soon sank in. He realized that the utopian disposition of ambitious architects needed to first square with the brutal reality of the real world; the dream world, in which students of architecture are schooled and immersed, needed to interface with the actual world to achieve some degree of parity. For those holding tenaciously onto the pristine dream world, unwilling to compromise, the way out of the quagmire of disconnect or ill fit was to seek a third space. So, Tong Jun parted ways, in career paths and with his college roommate and soulmate, Liang Sicheng (1901–1972). The two UPenn alumni were equally well-trained, ambitious, and motivated. Liang opted to launch his architect's career in the north. With Greek temples as his measuring rod, Liang was bent on finding Chinese equivalents in surviving historical monuments. He was also eager to materialize this "monumental" aspiration into modernized brick-and-mortar reality. Tong Jun chose a different route; he declined the invitation to stay in northern China. Not that Tong Jun was averse to monumentality. He shared Liang's monumental vision. In fact, he held the "monumental dream" to his bosom, literally.

The copy of Sir Banister Fletcher's *A History of Architecture on the Comparative Method* he owned was repeatedly in danger of being lost to his constant turmoils. On one occasion, when he and his family were fleeing to Beiping (today's Beijing), they were waylaid by train robbers who killed the train driver and left the train stranded in the wilderness. Tong Jun's brother, Tong Yin, took it upon himself to drive the train to its destination. Focused on a more vital task at hand, Tong Jun clutched close Fletcher's book and its accompanying slides. He was fine with the potential loss of all the luggage and belongings, but not that. The whole incident was uncanny, to say the least. The first edition of Fletcher's book features a photograph with the caption: "The Acropolis, Athens. With the Temple of Theseus in the foreground." But this caption is not entirely accurate. The Temple of Theseus actually occupies the middle ground. In the foreground are railroad tracks. It is as if Fletcher's *A History of Architecture on the Comparative Method*, in its 1896 edition, had already foretold the railroad episode of Tong Jun's story. It is as if Tong Jun's life was destined to enact the visual script already laid out in the 1896 edition of Fletcher's architectural history. Historical monuments, such as

9

those epitomized by the Temple of Theseus, are bound to recede into the background; and modern architects like Tong Jun face the reality of ruination, but they may hold on to their memory of these monuments. In the real world, they had to deal with the flux and the unrest of the changing reality, which the railroad tracks epitomize.

Tong Jun decided to go south. North versus south is a perennial divide in Chinese history. North is traditionally muscular, lordly, expansive, and controlling; south is sensitive, freewheeling, imaginative, and liberal. In the time when Tong Jun made the decision to go south, northern China was in the grips of northern warlords. Tong Jun couldn't quite understand Liang's decision to stay in the north. On one occasion, in 1930, Liang had pleaded with the northern warlords to leave a centuries-old bell tower along a road in Shenyang alone in their development plan. He had submitted an alternative plan in which the traffic could be rerouted without disturbing the tower; however, the warlords turned a deaf ear to Liang's impassioned plea, roughshod over his plan, and destroyed the tower nonetheless. That overbearing lordliness drove Liang to distraction. Despite that, Liang chose to stay in the north. Befuddled by Liang's decision, Tong Jun chose to go south.

Tong Jun came to Shanghai in 1931, where he and his UPenn alumni, Zhao Shen (1898–1978) and Chen Zhi (1902–2002) co-founded The Allied Architects (1932–1952), a private Chinese architecture firm. It was sandwiched between two overpowering sectors: the foreigners' firms and the government-controlled sector. Customers seeking trendiness gravitated toward the former; big-ticket projects were monopolized by the latter. The firm nevertheless eked out its existence between the two competing sectors. The Shanghai Mercantile Bank Building, built in 1933, exemplified the early style of The Allied Architects and bears Tong Jun's design thinking. The bank closed in 1937 as the Sino-Japanese War broke out. In the same year, Tong Jun turned his thoughts elsewhere. He seemed to have lost interest in monumental buildings. It was the burden that he, Liang Sicheng, and the whole generation of architects carried. They were obsessed with finding architecture worthy of Chinese civilization. They were fully cognizant of the European perception about China's lack of monumental buildings worthy of the Chinese civilization. James Fergusson (1808–1886), for one, in his classic *History of Indian and Eastern Architecture* (1876), certainly holds this view. This became an albatross that Tong Jun's generation carried on their backs. Liang was looking left and right in the north for monumental architecture worthy of Chinese civilization that was on par with Greek temples. In Liao architecture, he felt he had found it. Meanwhile, Tong Jun gave up monumentality. For him, Chinese culture was better epitomized in traditional gardens. With that, he had finally got that albatross off his back. "The Chinese garden," he opined, "is never meant to be monumental." But it stood tall among civilizations and held its court in comparison with European traditions. So, in the spring of 1937, when the Sino-Japanese War broke out, Tong Jun produced his *On Classical Gardens in Southeastern China*.

Like numerous other episodes of Tong Jun's life, his manuscript went through impossible situations. Tong Jun had entrusted the manuscript to the Society for Research in Chinese Architecture (SRCA), who had placed it in the storage room of the Chartered Bank in Tianjin. A flood submerged the bank storage, engulfing everything stored therein. Zhu Qiqian (1872–1964), the director of the Society, already advanced in years, plunged into the water and recovered the manuscript against all odds, but it had still gotten mangled by water and left barely legible. It was not until 1963 that it was finally published. The story of its recovery is uncannily consistent with the circumstances that prompted Tong Jun to write the book. Witnessing the deterioration and dilapidation of old garden sites, he took it upon himself to be its chronicler. In old gardens, he found his spiritual home.

For anyone steeped in architectural training in architectonic order and regularities, the Chinese garden is an acquired taste. It stands in sharp contrast with what architecture stands for. Largely antithetical to orderliness, symmetry, and regularity, its disposition is freewheeling, whimsical, and unshackled. It amounts to any individual seeking to break away from the regimented world. Naturally, it spoke to Tong Jun. To some extent, the chronicled gardens of southern China remain Tong Jun's best material biography.

Yet gardens are silent. Their modus operandi is understatement and reticence. They at once say everything and nothing. It is only fitting that Zhang Qin, an architect herself, who knows the Tong family intimately, ushers us into the labyrinth of Tong Jun's world—gardens and all—where we can sense Tong Jun's presence with immediacy and sensitivity. In between Zhang's lines are Tong Jun's footsteps and heartbeats. The reader experiences Tong Jun's garden through Zhang's prose, and vice versa.

Eugene Wang
June 22, 2023, Harvard University, Cambridge, Massachusetts

— FOREWORD —

T.S. Eliot's "The Hollow Men" ends with the lines, "This is the way the world ends … Not with a bang but a whimper." As a biographer, I am curious what Tong Jun, a poetry lover, would have thought about his world. The years of his life, from 1900 to 1983, were the most violent, and was also a turbulent era in the history of contemporary China.

Tong Jun was among one of the Chinese architects who studied overseas during the 1920s who played a prominent role in the development of their profession in the subsequent decades. However, his name is far from being known in contemporary China, let alone outside of China. The present volume is focused on the last twenty years of Tong Jun's life. It does not offer a full biography, nor does it survey his important design projects. Nevertheless, through this limited account of events and circumstances, it might be possible to gain a sense of much wider historical processes. When I began writing this book, I was motivated by my curiosity about Tong Jun. I sent the book to press with an even stronger sense of curiosity. My readers may emerge from reading this work with a similar sense of curiosity, new unresolved questions, but also a broader understanding. In this sense, we would have a real encounter on the path of curiosity; I suppose that we would share a common curiosity about China and about life beyond one's own familiar surroundings and national boundaries. I suppose that there will always be readers devoted to exploring and understanding distant countries and strange communities in an attempt to enrich their own lives. Tong Jun himself was also like this, taking in his stride differences in languages and cultures, finding resonances with others in a full life. During the Cultural Revolution, he gave an account of himself by saying that he was cosmopolitan.

Most of the world is no stranger to World War I, World War II, and the period of economic depression in between. The four years of civil war following World War II and successive brutal political campaigns in communist China may be a history too complicated and opaque for people outside mainland China. However, without understanding what happened in the past one hundred years, it is impossible to understand what is happening in China today, and what will be China's prospects in the future. I believe that the present volume will be accessible to readers who know little of Chinese history, as well as Chinese historians. In fact, I believe that this book will be a shortcut for readers wishing to gain a sense of China, this ancient and giant country.

Tong Jun was only in the U.S. for five short years, but the country left a deep and lasting impression on him. He had been studying English since elementary school, and his writing level was outstanding among native English speakers. When he arrived in America in 1925, Tong Jun felt at home right away. However, after he returned to China in 1930, he never had the opportunity to venture abroad again. In 1981, fifty-one years after he left the shores of America, he made the following inscription in an album of his paintings that was presented to his alma mater, the University of Pennsylvania. "As '*un ancien*,' I recall my school days in Phila., With proud nostalgia and deep gratitude." Throughout his working life, Tong Jun regularly wrote in English. His first essay published in China was composed in English, and the last book he completed was also written in English. This is a monograph on Chinese classic gardens: *Glimpses of Gardens in Eastern China*, which was published fifteen years after his death. Tragically, most readers in the English-speaking world are unaware of his almost desperate efforts to let the world know about Chinese architecture and gardens. I hope this book is a comfort to Tong Jun, as well as many Chinese intellectuals like him.

From the age of fifty onwards, Tong Jun was repeatedly forced to engage in writing "confessions" that criticized and denied himself. He wrote that he was "a thorough individualist who did not follow others and who did not follow populist trends. Someone who 'perfected himself in solitude'." He also summed up his life in the following way in a Cultural Revolution self-criticism document:

> *I was born into a bourgeois family and was nurtured*
> *on feudal thought as a child. As an adult, I received the*
> *enslavement education of American imperialists, and was*
> *particularly fond of capitalist culture, arts, and science*
> *and technology, as well as Chinese classical literature*
> *and art, immersing myself in it until it became elemental*
> *nature. Treating it as a foundation to lead a settled life, I*
> *developed a penchant for favoring the old and worshipping*
> *the foreign.*

In the period of greatest adversity, when he was made to kneel before the school where he taught, he murmured to himself, "*Eppur si mouve*" (and yet it moves). This was the line that Galileo had murmured to himself when he knelt before the Holy See. In this sense, there will always be people who can traverse long centuries and find their kindred spirits. In this sense, even when someone has been forgotten or consistently dismissed and overlooked, a brief account of his story may yet convey his indominable spirit.

I would like to express my thanks to Howard Goldblatt, the translator of my work. He helped me understand why English readers should know the story of Tong Jun and why they should have the opportunity of reading my work. Thanks also to the families of Tong Jun (Tong Linsu, Zhan Hongying, Tong Linbi, Gu Danyun, Tong Wei, Tong Wen, Tong Ming) and Liang Sicheng (Liang Zaibing, Yu Kui, Yu Xiaodong, Liang Jian, Annie Liang Zhou), to others who allowed me to interview them (Xiang Bingren, Fang Yong, Liu Guanghua, Wu Liangyong, Lin Zhu, Liu Xujie), and to Liu Guanghan, Zhou Wentao, Zhu Ning, Stanislaus Fung, Georgia (Gina) Tsarouhas, Chandranie, and Wang Chenhui and her team for their kind assistance in the creation and publication of this book.

—Zhang Qin

To Ilha Niohuru

— CHAPTER ONE —

"Out, Out, Brief Candle"

March 28, 1983, an ordinary day. Tong Jun's last day on Earth.

In March 1983, the city of Nanjing (China) bid goodbye to the bitter cold of winter as spring flowers began to bloom, indicating the approach of the best season of the year.

Right after an early lunch on March 28, Xiang Bingren,[2] a PhD student at then Nanjing Institute of Technology (present-day Southeast University) went to the hospital to relieve his fellow student, Fang Yong. Ever since his PhD advisor had been admitted, he and Fang Yong, who was pursuing his master's in architecture, had been taking turns at Tong Jun's bedside. But that day, he did not get to see his teacher.

No one, including Tong Jun himself, had expected that the Angel of Death would come knocking that day. He had, in fact, felt better the day before—to everyone's relief—and had even spent the morning going over the pages of his book manuscript. Unfortunately, shortly before noon, he took a turn for the worse.

His grandson, Tong Wen, had been in the room with him. Upon his alarmed exclamations, Tong Jun's younger brother, Tong Cun, rushed into the room and called for the doctor and nurse to attempt a last-minute resuscitation. At 12:26 in the afternoon, Tong Jun left us, holding the hand of his grandson, Tong Wen. When Tong Lingsu, Tong Jun's second son, and his wife arrived at the

1930, Tong Jun at Goethe House (Goethes Wohnhaus),
Frankfurt, Germany, during his Grand Tour to Europe

hospital after lunch, Tong Wen met them on the stairs. "Grandpa has passed away," he told his parents.

At the time, Zhan Yongwei, one of Tong Jun's former students from Nanjing Institute of Technology, who was also a former high school friend of Tong Jun's third son, Tong Linbi, was working at the Suzhou Gardens Bureau, and he chose with great care a slab of Suzhou granite for Tong Jun's grave marker. After talking it over at length, the family decided to carve only his name and dates on the stone. Tong Jun had once carved his own personal seal, which had said simply: Tong Jun, Architect. But, at the time of his death, he had not been an architect for over thirty years.

In May 1982, nearly a year before his death, Tong Jun had written in a letter to Wilma Fairbank, a friend and writer:

> *As to my personal health, you were so kind as to inquire. After all, I can say that chronic trouble typical of old age still does bother me much and that barring cancer and a traffic accident, the "brief candle" might yet take some time to be "out, out."*[3]

When viewed in retrospect, his light-hearted comment seems almost prophetic.

Tong Jun had discovered blood in his urine at the beginning of the year. Nearly twenty years earlier, in 1963, he had been diagnosed with bladder cancer, from which he had recovered fully after surgery. This unfortunate discovery clarified for him what it meant to have blood in one's urine. However, he was finishing work on his book and was racing against time. Wilma Fairbank was at that time also editing the collected writings of Liang Sicheng,[4] his friend and former colleague, who had died years before, for which she sought material from Tong Jun. In his letter to Fairbank, Tong Jun had quoted the following poetic lines from Shakespeare's *Macbeth*:

Out, out, brief candle!
Life's but a walking shadow, a poor player
That struts and frets his hour upon the stage
And then is heard no more: it is a tale
Told by an idiot, full of sound and fury,
Signifying nothing.[5]

Tong Jun often quoted Shakespeare. His love of Western literature and music lasted through all of his life. Whenever the pain from the late-stage cancer was unbearable, he would ask his grandson, Tong Wen, to read lines from Shakespeare to him. He forced himself not to moan as he listened. It was on one such day that the candle went out.

According to Qi Kang, Tong Jun's former student at Nanjing Institute of Technology, the last thing Tong Jun wrote was the "Jiangnan Yuanlin" entry in *Zhongguo Da Baike Quanshu* (*The Encyclopedia of China*).[6] He was still writing it in his sickbed. Once, when the doctor had come to give him an injection, he had said, "Give it to me in my leg, not my arm. That way I can keep writing."[7] But before he could finish what he was writing, his heart stopped beating.

Yan Longyu, an assistant assigned by the Communist Party of China to work with Tong Jun, also recalled in *Guanyu Tong Jun*:

> *At the time when Tong Jun was writing the "Jiangnan*
> *Yuanlin" entry, he could no longer walk, and did his*
> *writing in a recliner, with piles of books stacked beside*
> *him. Often, he would read a bit, write a few lines, and then*
> *lie back. In March, his condition deteriorated rapidly, and*
> *he could no longer eat. Often, he would be bent pressing*
> *down on his abdomen, as if to ease the pain; these were*
> *the times when it must have hurt the most. But as soon as it*
> *passed, he would write a little bit more.*[8]

Many years after Tong Jun's death, Xiang Bingren, now an old man, recalled Tong Jun with deep emotion in a personal interview with the author.[9] He candidly acknowledged the great gap in achievements between him, a student, and his academic advisor. He was Tong Jun's first PhD student at Nanjing Institute of Technology; in fact, his only one. After completing his master's degree, he'd begun a job search in Shanghai, China, looking forward to settling there, but once he started working, he found that gaining permanent residence in Shanghai for his wife was much harder than he'd thought it would be. China had just reinstated doctoral programs and students were being actively recruited, which was how he and Tong Jun had been fated to meet.

Xiang Bingren recalled how tense he was when he had to take the admission exam to become Tong Jun's doctoral candidate. He knew that a Japanese visiting scholar, Tanaka Tan, who had already written two books on Chinese architecture,[10] had once sought to become Tong Jun's graduate student. Tong Jun had asked him to translate into vernacular Chinese the "Zi Ren Zhuan" entry in the *Guwen Guanzhi* anthology[11] of classical Chinese essays, and then retranslate it into English. Tanaka had given up before he had even gotten started.[12] Still, Tong Jun had written a recommendation for him to study under Guo Husheng.[13] Tanaka later became a professor of classical Chinese architecture at Kyoto University, Japan. Xiang Bingren was aware of how hard it was to understand classical Chinese, let alone translate it into English. Fortunately for him, that was not the topic that Tong Jun tested him on. The examination paper he was given (according to Tong Wen's recollection[14]), listed the following five topics:

• Sketch the structure of the dome at Istanbul's Hagia Sophia Cathedral.

• Describe the "construction method" of Song Dynasty grand wooden structures.

• Draw Ludwig Mies van der Rohe's plan for the German Pavilion in the 1929 International Exposition in Barcelona (be specific).

• List all the construction projects you have participated in (do not make anything up).

• Discuss the design work with which you are most satisfied, and describe the essentials of that design and what you gained from it.

These seemed especially devised just for him, and so he easily passed. Xiang Bingren also recalls[15] the topics in his specialized courses:

• Expound on the relationship between cities and water sources.

• Examine and offer views of the Centre Pompidou in Paris.

• Analyze the curvature and flying eaves of rooftops on traditional Chinese buildings.

What was unusual was that Tong Jun had asked him if he had ever participated in architectural design, from the inception of a project to practical completion, and, if so, what he'd learned from the experience.

However, Xiang Bingren's application to the PhD program was inexplicably stopped by the university. Years later, Qi Kang told him that when Tong Jun, who had never asked anyone for a favor, learned of the rejection, he took his student's case to the university board, which led to Xiang becoming New China's first PhD candidate in architecture. In his seventies by then, Tong Jun was eager to take on a student to whom he could pass down what he himself had learned.

However, after being admitted, Xiang was distraught to learn that he indeed would have to translate the *Guwen Guanzhi* essays into English. Tong Jun handed him a list of essays from the anthology and had him come to his house bi-weekly to read them aloud and discuss them.

Tong Jun had also recommended eleven essays of the *Guwen Guanzhi* for his grandson Tong Wen to study; the first six were to serve as lessons on living, and the last five as windows to the human spirit. When I asked fifty-year-old Tong Wen if he could still recite any of these essays from memory, with a sheepish smile he replied that Tong Jun firmly believed that an architect needed both knowledge and morality. These essays taught the importance of being a moral human being, though that was a difficult lesson for students to grasp and accept, given the historical climate of those times. Tong Wen today is a scientist who has gained considerable fame in the field of radio transmission. But when he talks about his grandfather, he blushes, feeling unworthy, just like Xiang Bingren.

When studying under Tong Jun, Xiang Bingren and Fang Yong both took pains to avoid their somber, unsmiling advisor; they had even requested to change their twice-weekly tutorials to just once a week, and even that instilled trepidation in them. Whenever he recalled those days, Xiang was struck by the vast intellectual gap that existed between him and his advisor.

"I did not realize that not everyone has what it takes to be a scholar until I was much older. Most people have mediocre intellects, and while we have our minor accomplishments, we lack what it takes to be a scholar."[16]

He added that most people could not expect to reach the heights of his teacher, Tong Jun.

Tong Wen shared that the five research topics Tong Jun had proposed to Xiang Bingren were:

1. Studies of Frank Lloyd Wright (with Liu Guanghua,
Tong Jun's colleague, as co-advisor)

2. Architectural design (with Zhong Xunzheng[17])

3. Architectural environment (with Qi Kang)

4. The modern history of Shanghai architecture (with Yan Longyu)

5. Japanese architecture (with Guo Husheng)

Tong Jun preferred that Xiang Bingren undertake research on the modern history of Shanghai architecture because that was his field. But there were also concerns that people may consider him biased should he unwittingly monopolize the conversation; moreover, should he be unclear in any way, later generations may even accuse him of compounding errors. Tragically, Tong Jun fell seriously ill before the year was out, and died before Xiang graduated, forcing him to seek out another advisor in order to complete his degree requirements. However, no matter who he would have chosen, Xiang would quite possibly have found it difficult to wholeheartedly accept that person as his tutor.

Once the first generation of architects who had witnessed modern Shanghai architectural history began to die off, nothing would come to be produced at the turning point in this key historical moment of Chinese architectural history.

When Tong Jun died in Bed 207, on the second floor of the western wing of the Nanjing Regional Military General Hospital— though he was writing to the very end and was the author of numerous published works—he left no final testament. Not a word. Once known as the Central Hospital of Nanjing, the Nanjing Regional Military Hospital had been designed by his good friend, Yang Tingbao. Tong Jun had once playfully dubbed the main building an "upside-down bench."

Thirty years later, in recalling Tong Jun at a lecture in Shanghai,[18] Fang Yong shared that at the time Tong Jun's health deteriorated, he held no official government position or place of employment, and as such was denied admission to a hospital ward. Fortunately, Dr. Wang Tingfang,[19] who was a close family friend of Tong Jun's, worked at the Nanjing Regional Military General Hospital and advised Tong Jun's family to have him admitted there for emergency treatment. He was quickly given a bed and sent to surgery. During his stay there, he was cared for by no member of the hospital staff, nor any colleagues from the university. It was his students and family members who took turns attending to him. When Yang Tingbao returned from a work trip, he went right away to visit his old friend and see how Tong Jun was recovering from the surgery. Both men were optimistic enough to talk about work, and even of hosting Wilma Fairbank for a trip she was planning to China.

1982, Tong Jun in the Tsinghua University Architecture Department

The two elderly men's fates seemed bound together, for, less than a month later, Yang Tingbao suffered a cerebral haemorrhage and was admitted to the hospital for emergency treatment. A striking difference between the situations of the two friends was that Yang occupied important positions in government and academia, and received treatment befitting a provincial-level official. Ironically, Yang's request to be admitted to the Nanjing Military Regional General Hospital (which he himself had designed) in order to be near his friend was denied. The moment Tong Jun had recovered from his operation and was about to be transferred to the following radiology curation, he hastily told his second son, Tong Linsu, to ride a trishaw and take him to the hospital where his friend was admitted. Yang, who had just gained consciousness, was thrilled to see Tong, but colleagues who were in the room, on seeing how excited the two old men were, only allowed them to hold hands to keep them from getting too emotional. The two friends did not speak at their tearful reunion. Not long after this meeting, they both took leave of this world.

Tong Jun said something at the first session of a new term that was a great influence on Fang Yong throughout his life. He counseled future architects with these words:

> *A good architect must first be a good intellectual; only someone capable of independent thinking, with a rigorous scholarly approach, and an upright character, can create high-quality designs.*[20]

Fang Yong was perplexed by the unconventional way his advisor dealt with society and how he unusually accepted life in straitened circumstances—something that stayed with him well into his own later years.

On the thirty-fourth anniversary of Tong Jun's death, his granddaughter, Tong Wei, wrote a poem in honor of her grandfather:

"OUT, OUT, BRIEF CANDLE"

To An Architect

He is, the master architect letting go of the marble, to rise,
Carefully hammering, he chiseled the stone, to ascend,
Sculpting, artfully, he did not compete with the world

So-called perfection cannot come down from the top of an
arch bridge
Or through an arched gate, to enter Monet's Garden,
With both hands he encircled garden and architecture
As if united without seams

As if decided, on 1983, March 28, 12:26,
He separated perfection from the debris, then turned and left;
All the full-formed stones like idols
Began to return triumphant.

Seaside stone benches and Chinese gardens in the ocean of
his mind
Eroded into the sound of the evening prayer bell
Then, across the most arduous distance,
Reached for "the black hole,"

"Seen" the next day, 18 years too late.
He left before the black hole was discovered.
The black hole resides at the center of the Milky Way;
I live at the brim of his memory
Still feeling the violent gravity
Better suited to the distance of memory.

Our ancestors and Emperor Qin Shihuang's terra cotta
warriors
At the entrance of the tomb

Their insights long ago—spirits, absorbing gold and silver
Have shaped the architect's design;
Souls, turned jade into the architect's key, also his lock

No need to disturb the burial ground
Sooner or later,
All will grow the long, thick hair of the shade trees

Softly drowning, the tree fruits in love;
This morning, he came back, looking up
A cough from the indigo sky.[21]

— CHAPTER TWO —

The Chime Clock

One day, midway through the year 1982, Tong Jun sat in his usual spot in the Nanjing Institute of Technology reference room, reading a book.

Tong Jun led a very disciplined life, leaving his residence in Wenchang Lane (Nanjing) for the half-hour walk to the university (Nanjing Institute of Technology), where he read books and jotted down notes. As time passed, instructors and students in the Architecture Department became used to seeing the familiar figure sitting in the same spot. Occasionally, a student would ask him a question; sometimes he would answer on the spot, at other times, he'd write down the question to respond later. He called himself a clock, possibly either because he was as punctual as a clock, or because he sat in the same spot each day, day after day, like a desk clock, or even maybe because he had little to say other than to respond to questions—like a bell that sounds off only when it is struck. During the Cultural Revolution,[22] on one of the times when Tong Jun was asked to hand over "confessional material," he wrote:

In 1962, I told young instructors in the teaching and research group, "Develop the skill of asking questions and raising issues. Take a bell, for instance: if you strike it hard, it rings out loudly; if you strike it gently, it rings out softly; and if you don't strike it, it makes no sound."[23]

1924, Tong Jun studying at Beijing's Tsing Hua College (later renamed Tsinghua University)

That was how he encouraged students to ask questions.

Tong Jun was known as a "living dictionary." When faculty and students in the Architecture Department needed answers to academic questions, they went to Tong Jun. Yan Longyu recalled:

A particular table and chair in the periodicals room was Tong Jun's constant companion and the site where students, researchers, and instructors in the department went with their questions. He never felt put upon by people who came with questions, and whatever the subject—Chinese or foreign; ancient or modern; architecture to art; literature to history—he had answers. For foreign words that did not appear in common dictionaries, he would explain them by way of anecdotes or narratives in which they appeared. If asked a question he could not answer for the moment, he never tossed off a careless or evasive response, but would find the answer and then give it to the person who had asked the question.[24]

Fang Yong also recounted[25] one instance when a student had come to Tong Jun with a question he did not know how to answer. Fang Yong, who witnessed the incident, was stunned to see his teacher get red in the face. He was moved to discover that his teacher had an almost childlike innocence.

In early 1982, following his graduation from the architecture department at Nanjing Institute of Technology, Fang Yong was admitted into Tong Jun's master's program in architectural history. He was the first person admitted into the program after passing an entrance exam with questions from his future teacher. According to Fang Yong, only after he began his studies was Tong Jun paid at the highest salary tier for a professor.

Professor Tong's teaching method was to schedule meetings with his students to discuss topics. He did not

Top: 1980, Tong Jun in the living room of his Nanjing
residence at 52 Wenchang Lane
Bottom: Tong Jun speaking publicly in the Nanjing Institute
of Technology Research Center

*begin by giving me a reading list, but wanted me to read
widely. During the meeting, I was expected to ask as many
questions as possible, which he would unfailingly answer.
At first, we met two afternoons a week in the living room
of his Nanjing house at 52 Wenchang Lane, Taiping South
Road. I was both elated and somewhat uncomfortable.*

*Professor Tong sat there looking quite serious, and after
a detailed response to one question, waited patiently for
the next one. It is embarrassing to admit that I was nearly
thirty and did not have an adequate scholarly foundation
to continue conversing with him. Overwhelmed by the
pressure, I asked to meet only one afternoon a week,
despite my reluctance to miss out on half my opportunities
to learn. Professor Tong immediately thought of ways
to help me get up to speed; first was by reading two
books:* Guwen Guanzhi *and H.G. Wells's* The Outline of
History.[26, 27]

More than thirty years later, Fang Yong cited the words of
Zhu Xi from his *Yiluoyuan Yuanlu*[28] when remembering his study
sessions with Tong Jun: "Guangting[29] sat in a spring breeze for a
month," he said, recalling how those sessions at 52 Wenchang Lane
were like a breath of fresh air; a new start in life almost.

"I was so fortunate to be studying with Professor Tong, from
whom I learned both what to read and how to read."

These were the 1982 entrance exam topics for graduate
students pursuing their Master of Arts at Nanjing Institute of
Technology:

• Using the Beijing Qing-style method, make a one-
dimensional drawing and elevation of a Buddhist temple
roof and draw a front elevation (to scale). (25 percent)

• Discuss the spatial arrangement of groups of ancient Chinese buildings. (25 percent)

• When did the Renaissance begin? In which country and which city? Who are representative figures in the field of architecture? What were their works? (25 percent)

• How many floors are there in China's soon-to-be-completed tallest building? Where is it; what is its function? Where is the world's tallest building; how many floors? (Radio towers do not count). (25 percent)

Tong Jun was eighty-two at the time, long retired as an educator, yet still devoted to the education of his graduate students. To his regret, he had never been able to find suitable assistants and graduate students. In his later years he referred to himself as a "chiming clock," believing that there would be no one to follow in his footsteps if he didn't "chime." He was committed to passing on the fruits of his scholarly research to the next generation.

His grandson, Tong Wen, a sophomore in the Radio Communications Department at Nanjing Institute of Technology, often went to see him in his Architecture Department office. When he went there one day, Tong Jun said, "Let's go home"—something Tong Wen had never heard his grandfather say before. Tong Jun left his college office early with his grandson, taking the road he'd traveled for decades. Back home, he told his son, Tong Linsu, to contact his old friend, Dr. Wang, at the Nanjing Regional Military General Hospital and inform him that his body was acting up. He had noticed blood in his urine since the beginning of the year, but had told no one. On this day, he'd discovered blood clots in his urine and felt that his health was deteriorating. All this time, he had been a model of optimism since the initial diagnosis of bladder cancer in 1963, never uttering a word about death or funeral arrangements; he also hadn't taken a single day off work. So this time, his family was convinced that he would soon again

Tong Jun and Tong Cun at home

recover completely, feeling confident the same way they'd felt after his earlier surgery; all but his second brother, Tong Cun, a medical doctor, knew only too well what this latest development meant. As it turned out, Tong Jun never returned to the college—Nanjing Institute of Technology (which was at one time Central University)—where he had worked nonstop since the end of the war. The "clock" would never again be perched on the chair in which he'd sat for thirty years.

Tong Jun was the oldest of three brothers. He was especially close to his second brother, Shanghai resident Tong Cun, with whom he was regularly in touch. Tong Cun was an eminent medical scientist, an expert in microbiology and in antibiotics, and a graduate of Yenching University Preparatory School, Beijing, China, with doctorates in medicine from Beijing Union Medical College and public health from America's Johns Hopkins University. In 1946, he returned to China from America and, starting from scratch, led the backward, deficient pharmaceutical corps contingent in developing the People's Republic of China's very own penicillin, saving the lives of untold numbers of China's citizens; he also discovered erythromycin. He was China's trailblazer in the field of antibiotics. As soon as he heard about the state of Tong Jun's health, he rushed to Nanjing from Shanghai.

Tong Jun was admitted to the hospital to undergo a series of tests in July 1982. He was operated on a month later, at a time when he was burning with impatience: "Let's hurry up and get this over with, I need to get better fast. There's so much to do."[30] He asked to have his manuscripts, books, correspondence, and dictionaries brought to his hospital bed, where he continued to write, even on the day of his cystoscope test. He was oblivious to the agony Tong Cun felt, for the test results showed that the cancer was in its late stages, and had begun to metastasize. Upon consulting a few colleagues at Nanjing Regional Military General Hospital, Tong Cun had no illusions regarding the gravity of his brother's condition; afraid that nothing more could be done, he needed to decide if more surgery was called for, and if so, what sort. He told no one how serious it was. The subsequent operation—which had initially offered one last ray of hope—tragically revealed what he had feared. Upon discovering that the cancer had spread too far, the surgeon called Tong Cun into the operating room, seeking his opinion on what to do. Helplessly, this leading authority in his field realized that his brother's case was hopeless; all he could do was swallow his agony and tell his colleague, "Sew him up."[31]

After the operation, Tong Jun was confident that he was on the road to recovery—a repeat of 1963—and so he refused his brother's tactful suggestions that he prepare for the inevitable. But he may have had an idea of what the future held, for he threw himself into his work, hardly resting, day or night. Just ten days after the surgery, he was proofreading the pages of *Zao Yuan Shi Gang (The Outline of Garden History)*[32] sent to him by China Architecture & Building Press. He was also working on his own book manuscript. Owing to his post-operative frailty, he worked sitting up in bed, beads of perspiration dripping from his head, his hand shaking, dictating to a student assistant between gasping breaths, word by word, sentence by sentence, to complete the manuscript of tens of thousands of words.

Huang Yiluan, secretary of the Party Branch of the Department of Architecture recalled how the elderly Tong Jun perspired heavily from the pain he suffered, but he never shed a tear, never moaned, never despaired, never displayed feelings of pessimism, and never let his expression show what he was going through. When the pain became unbearable, he just forced air out in rapid puffs, minus the cries, repeating over and over: "I need to get better fast. There's so much to do." Even with tubes stuck in his arms, he never stopped reading newspapers and research material.[33]

When Tong Wen accompanied him to the hospital for a follow-up check-up after his surgery, they talked about the forthcoming publication, *Dongnan Yuanshu (Glimpses of Gardens in Eastern China)*.[34] Tong Jun was without a qualified assistant for a long time, so after finishing the manuscript, he let Tong Wen type up two of the chapters, after which he asked his grandson what he thought. Tong Wen said he didn't understand what his grandfather had written and wondered why he'd written it in the first place. How many people would read it? And how many of those who did would understand it? After he'd asked the questions, Tong Wen felt his grandfather grip his hand tightly, and sensed his body shake violently. A long moment passed before he said: "People who come after us will be smarter than we are." Thirty years later, Tong Wen recalled this episode and said with a sigh: "He was so lonely and so fiercely unconventional."[35]

Dongnan Yuanshu (Glimpses of Gardens in Eastern China), Tong Jun's study of gardens, was written in English. Its scholarly importance surpassed his book published in 1963 on the study of Chinese gardens, *Jiangnan Yuanlin Zhi (On Classical Gardens in*

Southeastern China),[36] which he wrote in his thirties. *Dongnan Yuanshu,* however, is a product of his later years, after decades of accumulated knowledge through research. Chinese garden design is a synthetic art, and only someone like Tong Jun, who was well-schooled in both Chinese and Western cultures, could write a masterpiece like *Dongnan Yuanshu.* Like all his other work, it displays his style of sparse prose. In regard to that style of writing, Zhu Guangya[37] shared:

> *Back when I read Tong's essays, it was like gnawing on hardtack. Every paragraph overflowed with information, which took a long time to digest. Now that I can read Tong Jun's jottings, I can finally see how he was able to accomplish that. The pages are packed with his minute script, totally devoid of groundless speculations and sensationalism; it was like sifting through sand to pick out gold nuggets—a process that lasted decades—to the point where his scholarly knowledge covered both concrete aspects and abstract concepts, and merged East and West, leaving the impression that "the floating clouds could not obscure his views, because he was positioned at the highest possible vantage point."*[38]

The genesis of *Dongnan Yuanshu* can be traced back to when Tong Jun hosted a team of European representatives somewhere after 1977 to 1978. He had remarked that the foreigners actually believed that Chinese gardens were essentially Japanese imports. Tong Wen recalled him saying:

> *I wanted to write something because of the paucity of published works on the subject, while the Japanese had written volumes on this subject, which is why the foreigners assumed that Chinese gardens were directly influenced by Japan, which is a total reversal of the facts.*

My plan was to write a booklet, so I contacted tourist
agencies and government tourism offices in order to reach
out to more people.[39]

This is probably why he wrote the book in English. At the
time, though, China was just opening up to the world, and no
publisher outside of China would possibly publish the book, and
in China, the number of expert garden researchers who could read
English texts was minuscule. From the birth of the booklet, up
until today, Tong Jun's hope for the text has not yet been realized—
which is to get the booklet in the hands of every member of tourist
groups. By the same token, while the Suzhou gardens (Jiangsu
Province) are listed as a World Heritage Site, the cultural and
artistic value of China's gardens are nowhere near as well-known
in the West as their Japanese counterparts. Thus, the value of this
booklet has not achieved wide enough recognition.

Well-known Chinese architect Wang Shu,[40] nearly sixty years
Tong Jun's junior, was one of the earliest readers of the booklet.

My attitude toward China's classic gardens in the south
changed from that of "the same old story"—something that
had lost all meaning in the modern day—to one of renewed
enthusiasm and interest. If I were to say that reading the
earlier Tong Jun Wenxuan (Selected Works of Tong Jun)[41]
was a warm-up, then reading the 1996 first edition of
Dongnan Yuanshu *in the Chinese translation comprised a*
true conceptual turning point. There was one particular
sentence that struck me when reading the book in 1996,
where I could barely contain my amazement; a loud buzz
went off in my head.[42]

The sentence that struck such a deep chord was a question
with regards to rocks used to make realistic hills in a garden, but
for Wang Shu, it was a moment of enlightenment. Wang Shu has

admitted openly that Tong Jun's writing actually changed his personality and taught him how to be calm and gentle.[43]

The publishing of *Dongnan Yuanshu* involved many twists and turns. Not long before Tong Jun's passing, Yang Yongsheng, a publisher,[44] went to see him in Nanjing with plans to reissue *Jiangnan Yuanlin Zhi*, and had asked him about publishing more books. Tong Jun told him he was writing a study of gardens in English, making clear that it was not going to be an English translation of *Jiangnan Yuanlin Zhi*. He also revealed that he was writing a synopsis on the rise of modern and contemporary Chinese architecture; another planned book, which would deal with theories and the history of urban planning, was to be a hefty volume. Yang Yongsheng advised against publishing his English manuscript with China Architecture & Building Press, but to send it to SDX Joint Publishing in Hong Kong instead.

After Tong Jun's death, Yang returned to Nanjing and informed Tong Jun's family that at the time, he had actually wanted to recommend to Tong Jun that *Dongnan Yuanshu* be published by International Press in Beijing, the publisher of (his friend) Liu Dunzhen's[45] *Classical Gardens of Suzhou (Suzhou Gudian Yuanlin).*[46] But since Tong Jun had no "official" government title, that possibility was closed to him. However, his English preface titled "Suzhou Gardens"[47] for Liu's *Classical Gardens of Suzhou* that was published by SDX Joint Publishing had been well received. The publisher was so taken by the work that they had requested Yang to submit all of Tong Jun's work to them, but sadly, by the time Yang proposed *Dongnan Yuanshu*, the publisher had died.

Dongnan Yuanshu sat on the back burner for the next ten years, not seeing print until 1997, when it was printed as part of an anniversary celebration by the Architecture Department at Southeast University. The original manuscript was handwritten; Tong Wen initially typed up only ten to twenty pages for his grandfather. It was a very slow process, which he abandoned when he got busy doing other things. After Tong Jun's death, his son, Tong Linsu, finished typing the manuscript during the summer break in July.

When Tong Jun was studying gardens in Southern China, he compiled a list of plant names. Yuan Yiwei helped him complete the portion of *Dongnan Yuanshu* on botanical research. She was the daughter of one of Tong Jun's neighbors in his Shanghai Anlecun apartment, and a favorite of Tong Jun's wife. Upon graduation Yuan Yiwei received a work assignment at Nanjing's Zhongshan Botanical Garden. While she worked there, Tong Jun and his wife took her in as an unofficial foster daughter, treating her as their own. She and her family dined with Tong Jun and his wife once a month until the Cultural Revolution. Matching Chinese plant names to their Western counterparts was groundbreaking work at the time, and Tong Jun insisted on including a mention of Yuan in his book to acknowledge her contribution.

Once, when Tong Wen went with Tong Jun for a physical exam, while they were on the road, he remarked, "If an artist has not made his mark by the age of twenty, his career is over. For an educator, it's thirty, a scientist, forty, and a politician fifty."

To that, Tong Jun responded:

An architect doesn't reach maturity before the age of fifty. Only then is he capable of architectural design that can stand the test of time. You're wrong in thinking that excellence in architecture relies primarily on artistry.[48]

At the age of fifty, Tong Jun, who was born in 1900, had lived during a special period in China's history, and in a special environment. In his 1944 essay "The Architectural Education," he wrote: "The greatest delight in life is gained from reading, but the happiest and most memorable days are those studying architecture."[49]

His professional life as an architect ended abruptly at the age of fifty, the age—according to him—when an architect matures.

Tong Jun embraced his loneliness with writing, from his middle years—when the desk clock was silenced—to his later years—when the chime clock rang out on its own—the only sound being in his writing, alone.

— CHAPTER THREE —

A Last Visit to Tsinghua

October 1982, Tong Jun traveled to Beijing for radiation treatment, his first visit to the capital in nearly thirty years. Beijing, formerly Beiping, played a significant role in Tong Jun's life. Upon his graduation from middle school, he took the entrance exam for Tangshan Chiao Tung University in Fengtian (now Shenyang). His father, the newly appointed Director of Education for Fengtian Province, had been sent to Beijing on official business, and there had learned that Tsing Hua College (later renamed Tsinghua University), a preparatory school for study in the United States, had, just that year, begun accepting applications from students in Northeast China. And so, on his father's advice, Tong Jun decided to try his luck. During those days, in order to improve his proficiency in English, he took refresher classes in English at Tianjin's Xinxue Academy. After taking the Tangshan Chiao Tung University entrance exam, he rushed to Beijing to sign up for the Tsing Hua College entrance exam. Among the three to four hundred hopefuls were five from the three northeastern provinces of China. Tong Jun had scored top in the Tangshan Chiao Tung University entrance exam and came in third in the Tsing Hua College entrance exam. When it came time to decide, he chose Tsing Hua College. He left his home in Shenyang and traveled to Beijing, ostensibly the first Tsing Hua College student ever from Northeast China.

1923, Tong Jun's senior year at Tsing Hua College,
Beijing, China

During his middle school days in Fengtian, Tong Jun had studied Western oil painting and pencil sketches. At Tsing Hua College, his art advisor was Miss Star; graced with extraordinary talent, and being the beneficiary of excellent teaching, Tong Jun quickly became a prominent character on the art faculty, and also became the art editor for the school magazine. His pen-and-ink drawings and watercolors were so well-known on campus that he had even put on a solo exhibition, and from 1922 to 1925, was the artistic editor of Tsing Hua College's yearbook. (Later, from 1925 to 1928, as a student at the University of Pennsylvania Architecture Department [United States], he also took first place in a watercolor contest.) At Tsing Hua College, besides his interest in art, he was also fascinated by "crew" (team) sports and joined the rowing team. Rowing requires a strong back and shoulders, and Tong Jun was actually a member of the college's competition team; however, his talent in this sport is seldom, if ever, mentioned.

Tsing Hua College was home to many distinguished individuals: Liang Qichao,[50] Wang Guowei,[51] Zhao Yuanren,[52] and Chen Yinque[53] were all on the faculty at the time. Wang Wenxian was one of Tong Jun's English professors; Mei Yiqi taught him physics; Bing Zhi was his biology professor; and John Ma was his athletics advisor. He frequently went to lectures by Liang Qichao, Hu Shi,[54] and Wang Guowei. No one had a greater influence on Tong Jun than Wang Guowei, whose advanced courses in Chinese literature were unquestionably his favorites. Wang, who was self-educated, created his own field of study, with breakthroughs in education, philosophy, literature, drama, aesthetics, history, and classics, among others. At Tsing Hua College, Wang reached the height of erudition—an expert, one could say, in all things ancient and modern, and East and West. The contents of his classroom lectures were like pearls of wisdom, and he won Tong Jun's unalloyed admiration. Even in Tong Jun's later years—as Tong Wen shared in correspondences with the author—he encouraged his grandson to study hard with lines from Wang's *Three Realms of Life*: "Last night, the west wind shrivelled jade-like green trees, alone I climbed the high tower to see the limit of roads that lead to the end of the world; my clothes and belt are getting loose, yet from beginning to end, I have no regrets. For her I languish, and become wan and sallow. I looked for her thousands of times in a crowd. Suddenly I turned around, and she was standing in a spot with fading lamplight."[55]

Wang Guowei was also Tong Jun's spiritual mentor. He had once given Tong Jun a list of recommended books, which he had kept with him for decades, in war and peace, losing them only when they were confiscated in a house search during the Cultural Revolution. It surely would have been longer, covering more than the list of essays from *Guwen Guanzhi* that Tong Jun prepared for his students.

Reading Tong Jun's *Jiangnan Yuanlin Zhi (On Classical Gardens in Southeastern China)*, we can see, vis-à-vis Wang

Guowei's *Renjian Cihua (Poetic Remarks on the Human World)*; while different in approach, they are similar in execution. By way of example, Wang had his popular "three realms of scholarship," while Tong Jun had his "three realms of gardens." Tong Jun began with an analysis of the word "garden," while for Wang, the word was "hall." Chen Yinque, Wang's colleague on the college's faculty commemorated Wang's death with the following inscription:

> *In the pursuit of learning, a True Scholar breaks the shackles of mundane values, for only thereby can he pursue the Truth. This Man chose to die rather than live on with his mind imprisoned. This, then, is the heart of the matter: this spirit of sacrifice is shared by all outstanding and sagacious individuals, be they in the past, or alive today. How can common folk hope to understand such things?*

> *It is through his death that This Man demonstrated an independent and free mind. His act was not occasioned by mere personal grievance, nor was it driven by dynastic collapse. It is in a mood of deep mourning that we have erected this stele near his lecture hall, expressing hereby our boundless sense of loss. And this stele represents the extraordinary qualities of this gentleman, one whose spirit is forever vouchsafed to vast Heaven above.*

> *The future cannot be known; indeed, there may come a time when this gentleman's work no longer enjoys pre-eminence, just as there are aspects of his scholarship that invite disputation. Yet, his was an independent spirit, and his mind unfettered—these will survive the millennia to share the longevity of Heaven and Earth, shining for eternity as do the sun, the moon, and the very stars themselves.[56]*

What Chen Yinque wrote illuminates the lasting influence Tsing Hua College exerted on Tong Jun: an independent spirit and free thinker.

Tong Jun at Tsing Hua College campus as a student

In the home of Tong Shibai, Tong Jun's first son
Back row, right: Tong Wei
Front row: Tong Jun

In addition to the star-studded line-up of teachers, there was also considerable brilliance among Tong Jun's fellow students at Tsing Hua College. He was on especially friendly terms with Wen Yiduo, possibly because Wen's younger brother, Wen Yiqi, was Tong Jun's classmate. Wen Yiduo, a renowned poet and intellectual, was one of the founders, along with Liang Shiqiu, of the Tsinghua Literature Society. Tong Jun was accomplished in literature, especially poetry. In the summer of 1978, he spent several days under a grape trellis in his rear garden typing a long letter to his eldest son, Tong Shibai, and his wife, Zheng Min. The poet Zheng Min was deeply moved when she read the letter, which was written in English. She told Tong Wen[57] that it was the most romantic piece she'd ever read; a revelation of his notion of love, written in the style of nineteenth-century novels.

Tong Jun's circle of friends included Liang Sicheng, Chen Zhi, and Huang Jiahua—all seniors who were two years ahead of him; classmate Cai Fangyin; and Lin Tongji, Guo Yuanxi, Ha Xiongwen, Liang Yan, Wang Huabin, and Huang Xueshi, all juniors, a year behind him. Zhang Zhizhong from the school's Art Society was also a close friend. The list of Tong Jun's classmates who studied abroad after graduating from Tsing Hua College totalled sixty-eight individuals, most of whom returned home after completing their overseas studies. Though they returned to a war-torn homeland and were caught up in political movements, experiencing a range of epochal and human adversities, many of them hung on to become leaders in their chosen fields, and precursors of future developments in China. In the "disclosure documents"[58] that Tong Jun submitted during the Cultural Revolution, he stated that during his stay in the United States, and after his return, his Tsinghua classmates and fellow students comprised his primary circle of social connections. There can be no doubt that Tong Jun was deeply influenced by his four years at Tsing Hua College, an influence that lasted throughout his life.

It was hard for all members of Tong Jun's family to gather for family reunions, even for major events such as marriages and funerals. One extremely rare family reunion occurred in 1982, while Tong Jun was in Beijing undergoing radiation treatment. He was staying in the home of his son, Tong Shibai; his third son, Tong Linbi, was working in the Ministry of Aerospace Industry also in Beijing. No one knew whether or not Tong Jun had a clear understanding of his condition, though he appeared to be in a positive frame of mind.

When he returned to Nanjing, he wrote to Wilma Fairbank, in which he was optimistic that he was on the road to recovery:

I came back last week from Peking [romanized from Beijing], where I received radioactive treatment from a

medical hospital, after the surgical removal of a tumor in
[my] bladder in Nanking [romanized from Nanjing]. Now
the cure is complete and I am feeling fine and am ready to
finish the work I started before I was sick.[59]

The truth is, Tong Jun never stopped working. He made
changes to the English manuscript of *Dongnan Yuanshu* from his
hospital bed during radiation sessions in Beijing. His suitcases
were mostly filled with books and manuscripts when he traveled
to Beijing. During his two months there, he subjected *Dongnan
Yuanshu* to a complete revision.

Writing about Tong Jun's trip to Tsinghua University, ninety-
year-old architect Wu Liangyong's recollections are unerringly
complete:

Accompanied by his eldest son, Tong Shibai, Tong Jun
made a trip to visit the Architecture Department at
Tsinghua University, where Tong Jun had a photograph
taken with his former students and the students of these
former students. Happy to see him, they asked him to speak.
Many Beijing alumni of Central University's Architecture
Department[60] *joined the reunion, and the vice-minister of*
the Housing and Urban-Rural Development, Dai Nianci,
a 1942 graduate of the Central University Architecture
Department, hosted a dinner.[61]

In his youth, Tong Jun enjoyed having his picture taken, but
in virtually every photo among the large stack he left behind, he is
stiff and expressionless. The photo taken that day was no different.
Tong Jun was seated in the center, his students standing behind him.
He wears a somber expression. It would be his last visit to Tsinghua
University and the last time he would participate in a public event.

Liang Sicheng's widow, Lin Zhu, recalled this visit to
Tsinghua in a personal interview with the author:

Top: 1982, Tong Jun at Tsinghua University Architecture
Department
Bottom: 1982, at Tsinghua University Architecture Department
Back row: Wu Liangyong (3rd from the left), Tong Shibai (first
on the right)

From a distance, I saw that he was surrounded by a large
group of professors. I knew he was one of Sicheng's close
friends, and was someone I respected as well. But no one
had told him who I was, and I had no opportunity to talk to
him. He seemed quite energetic, not at all like a man who
would soon pass away.[62]

Tong Jun once had his picture taken in Tong Shibai's home.
Tong Wei said: "A bookcase, an armchair, and some daffodils
served as the backdrop. Light came from the window in front of
my father's desk."[63]

Tong Jun's face was expressionless, giving him a solemn,
reserved look, as if he'd seen through all that the world had to
offer. Deep wrinkles hid memories of a hard life. He was lonely,
but at peace, a bit like an old peasant, and a bit like an enlightened
monk. It was the last photo he would ever take.

Despite the considerable influence Tsing Hua College had
on the young Tong Jun, in the early 1950s, when the university
established the architecture department, he turned down Liang
Sicheng's invitation to return to the campus and stayed in Nanjing,
where he would live out his life.

In his later years, Tong Jun summed up his relationship with
Tsinghua in two sentences:

If I had not chosen Tsing Hua College in 1921, and enrolled
instead at Tangshan's Chiao Tung University, I would
have died in the deadly Tangshan earthquake. If I had
chosen Tsinghua University in 1949, I would have died in a
struggle[64] *session during the Cultural Revolution.*[65]

Indeed, if he had accepted a teaching position at Tsinghua
University, he may well have suffered even more in the violent
storms of Beijing. But at the time, when the People's Republic was
founded in 1949, most individuals—Liang Sicheng, for instance—

enthusiastically welcomed the peaceful creation of New China. Who could have anticipated how the cruel political movements would alter China's destiny?

1982, Tong Jun at the home of Tong Shibai

— CHAPTER FOUR —

Revered Friend Yang Tingbao

In 1982, in Beijing, Tong Jun was devastated to learn that his friend Yang Tingbao had died.

Before Tong Jun left for radiation treatment in Beijing, his dear friend Yang Tingbao had been rushed to the hospital with a cerebral haemorrhage. He had made a special trip to the hospital with his son, Tong Linsu, to see Yang upon recovering from his surgery, and the two old men had clasped hands for a long moment, telling each other to take care. Neither expected that it would be their last meeting.

On January 15 the next year, Tong Jun wrote a commemorative piece for his friend titled "The Philosopher of a Generation Has Passed Away, Where Will I Find Another Who Knew Me so Well?"[66] Han Yu (762–824), a philosopher and litterateur in the Tang dynasty,[67] defined the term "*zhe ren*" (philosopher) as a "man of upright manner and unyielding temperament."[68] For us, a philosopher is someone with profound wisdom and a high moral standing. Tong Jun's essay was filled with fond memories, describing in detail many of his and Yang Tingbao's experiences together. The pages of his handwritten essay show traces of his tears. The final sentence of this memorial read: "Words cannot describe how deeply the passing of one of my dearest friends has hit this old man."

One gets the impression that there was so much more he wanted to say, but he knew that nothing could fully express the pain he felt, and so he ended on that note.

1934, Tong Jun and Yang Tingbao in Suzhou, China

Tong Linsu recalled :

On the day that he received word from Nanjing of Uncle Yang's death, Father stared at the fateful letter for a long time without saying a word, long sighs accompanied by tears. Then he asked me for a pen and paper, and began writing a memorial piece on his sickbed. He titled it "The Philosopher of a Generation Has Passed Away, Where Will I Find Another Who Knew Me so Well?" He spent the rest of that day in total silence.[69]

Tong Jun and Yang Tingbao were fellow alumni twice—
of Tsing Hua College and later, of the University of Pennsylvania
(UPenn). Their friendship began in 1925, when Tong Jun decided
to study architecture in the United States. In UPenn, schoolmates
like Liang Sicheng and Chen Zhi considered Yang a *weiyou* or
devoted friend, and a mentor of sorts. The term *weiyou* comes from
an essay by the Ming scholar Su Jun, in which he describes the
qualities of four types of friends, one of which is *weiyou*:

> *With a* weiyou *(esteemed friend), one's sense of morality and*
> *justice is sharpened, and one's errors are corrected; with a*
> miyou *(bosom buddy) one gets a hand at critical moments*
> *and trusts one's life when needed; with a* niyou *(an intimate*
> *friend), one hears honeyed words and has a great time*
> *seeking pleasure; with a* zeiyou *(contrary friend) all is well*
> *when on good terms, but one can turn after a falling out.*[70]

Yang Tingbao was one year younger than Tong Jun, but was
already enrolled in the University of Pennsylvania Architecture
Department, where his exceptional talents were widely recognized,
as was reflected in his superior grades. He was awarded first prize
in a nationwide student design contest, as well as a Municipal
Art Prize, Emerson Prize, Warren Prize, and many more of such
accolades. Zhu Bin,[71] Fan Wenzhao,[72] and Zhao Shen,[73] were also
students at the university at that time, and were soon followed
by Tong Jun, Chen Zhi,[74] Liang Sicheng, and Lin Huiyin.[75]
These creative, intelligent young men and women were such
accomplished students that they elicited compliments from their
American peers, like: "Damn clever, these Chinese!" and were
even known as the "Chinese contingent."[76]

When Yang Tingbao completed his undergraduate coursework
ahead of schedule, the *Philadelphia Evening Bulletin* ran a story
with the headline: "Chinese Student Yang Tingbao Graduates from
the University of Pennsylvania with Special Honors, Completing

Degree Requirements in Architecture in Less than Three Years."[77]
A year later, Yang received a Master of Arts (Architecture), with
some of his work featured in *American Exercises in Architectural
Designs.*[78] Upon graduation, he worked in the office of Paul
Philippe Cret (1876–1945), renowned American architect, who was
also his teacher at UPenn for a year. Contemporary photographs
of Yang show someone who had practiced martial arts since his
childhood, and who had now grown tall and strong; a handsome
man who always kept an upright posture and who often stood out
in a crowd.

In 1926, after the Grand Tour of Europe with Zhao Shen,
Yang Tingbao returned to China, where he joined Kwan, Chu
and Yang Architects & Engineers founded by Guan Songsheng (a
construction engineer and architect, and a track and field activist
who ardently promoted the sport in the Republic in the 1950s). In
1934, he traveled frequently to Shanghai for work.

Yang Tingbao in the office of The Tsing Hua Alumni Society

"There were many architects in Shanghai with whom we were friendly," Tong Jun wrote of Yang in his memorial, "but as a pair of northerners, we were especially close. We got together nearly every Sunday to visit places of historical interest in cities and towns in the Shanghai environs. On several occasions, we went to Luzhi (town) to see the Tang sculptures in Baosheng Temple, and to the Guyi Garden in Nanxiang. After a day's outing, we went back to my place in Shanghai for dinner. He was a frequent guest at my house. Sometimes, he went into the kitchen to make some noodles with eggs, a dish my wife referred to as 'Yang Tingbao noodles.' After dinner, we sat around talking. I'd sometimes take out recently purchased classical Chinese paintings or books for us to enjoy leafing through. My wife would say I was showing off our treasures again, a play on the word 'bao' in Yang's name."[79]

In the section on Yang Tingbao in Tong Jun's Cultural Revolution disclosures, he wrote:

Yang and I were students at Tsing Hua. I was admitted to the College in 1921, two years after he had left for overseas study in America. I learned that he was studying architecture. In 1925, I left for America to study in the University of Pennsylvania Architecture Department, from which he had already graduated and was working in Philadelphia. We met on Sundays from time to time. In 1927, he returned to China and went to work for Kwan, Chu and Yang Architects & Engineers in Tianjin as an architectural designer. I came home (to Shenyang) in 1930 to take up a teaching position in Northeastern University in Shenyang. We did not exchange letters during those years. In 1931, I left Shenyang and joined a private architectural firm in Shanghai as a partner (which became The Allied Architects in 1932). From that time

Yang Tingbao visiting Suzhou gardens, Jiangsu Province,
China, with Tong Jun

forward, we met up every time Yang Tingbao was sent from
Nanjing to Kwan, Chu and Yang Architects & Engineers'
Shanghai office, and we sometimes took in scenic sites in the
Shanghai environs.

We moved separately to Chongqing in 1938, each of us
continuing to work for our respective firms. I went from
Chongqing to Guiyang (Guizhou Province) in 1940,
but returned to Chongqing four years later to teach at
Shapingba National Central University's Architecture
Department. Around 1943, Yang was sent by the National
Resource Commission of the Chongqing Government on a
study tour to America. He returned to Chongqing in 1945,
where we once again met frequently. While I was working
in Guiyang, Yang Tingbao came to see me twice to do
some professional work for his office, staying each time for
about a week. We met both times. When things settled down
after victory in the War of Resistance,[80] we both wound
up back in Nanjing, busy with our own affairs. But before
long, he began teaching in National Central University's
Architecture Department; I still had classes to teach since
I joined the same university in Shapingba. We have met
nearly every day in the years since Liberation.[81, 82]

When Northeastern University planned to establish an
architecture department in 1928, Yang Tingbao was their choice
for department chair. But he had already signed on with Kwan,
Chu and Yang Architects & Engineers. Recent graduates Liang
Sicheng and Lin Huiyin were touring Europe at the time. Sicheng's
father, Liang Qichao, was trying to arrange for him to join the
faculty at Tsinghua University, but had heard nothing conclusive
from the university. When news of Northeastern University's plans
reached Liang Qichao, he asked Yang Tingbao to recommend

Liang Sicheng as the first chair of the newly created department. Yang was working on a number of important projects for Kwan, Chu and Yang Architects & Engineers, and despite the fact that he was the firm's pre-eminent architect, and the best known of all the firm's partners, he abided by the contract he had signed when he was hired, listing all his works under the firm's name instead of his own. After the war ended, Yang was hired by their mutual friend Liu Dunzhen as a professor of architecture at Central University (later Nanjing Institute of Technology), where he assumed the chairmanship after 1949. From then on, he and Tong Jun remained colleagues for the rest of Tong Jun's life.

In "Critique of the Architecture Research Group of Nanjing Institute of Technology" ("Dui Nangong Jianzhu Yanjiushi De Pipan"), Tong Jun wrote:

Yang Tingbao and I studied architecture at the same university in America, took the same courses, and shared both a lifestyle and, coincidentally, a point of view. There were never any disputes between us in terms of scholarship, techniques, or the arts, not because we wanted to be civil or were modest, but because we saw things the same way. When dealing with questions in the lab, if he proposed a solution, I invariably agreed without a second thought. I never suggested that his ideas were those of the bourgeoise, since I was unschooled in the tenets of socialism. We supported one another.[83]

In *Life Under a Scorching Sun,*[84] Liu Guanghua recalled:

After the thought reform movement, Liu Dunzhen invited everyone to a picnic at Xuanwu Lake [Nanjing, Jiangsu Province]; as people who shared similar views, we could talk freely, with no concern over scruples. But it wasn't much fun, so when someone suggested taking a trip to

Suzhou, many readily agreed. But [around the same
time] students and faculty of the architecture department
[of Nanjing Institute of Technology] were planning an
excursion, hoping that everyone would make the trip as
a group. That did not sound appealing, so Yang Tingbao
suggested that we meet on the train to Suzhou and take
rooms in a hotel, and if students asked, we'd each find an
excuse to miss their [planned] outing. We spent several
enjoyable days in Suzhou.[85]

From this, we can see the sort of atmosphere Yang Tingbao created as leader of the architecture department.

Fang Yong recalled[86] that in 1970, Yang Tingbao held a number of important positions, including "Vice Governor, Jiangsu Province" and "Chairman, Architecture Society Board." He kept busy with administrative matters and was often heard to mock himself, saying: "If I'm not in an oven, I'm in a freezer." He sometimes fell asleep while leading an evaluation session, saliva leaking out of the side of his mouth. Although he was a senior government official and a leader in professional organizations, he approached things along the motto, "Handle everything appropriately; be friendly to all without forming cliques." It formed the core of his conduct, and the foundation upon which he and Tong Jun built their friendship.

Tong Jun, on the other hand, held himself apart from such activities. He had been an architecture professor and scholar; he'd also served as an independent representative in the Kuomintang-Communist Political Consultation Conference in 1946 in Chongqing, but after the negotiations between the two parties broke down, he lost faith in politics and left it behind for good. In the 1950s, the Jiangsu provincial government invited him to serve as the head of the Building Department. He did not respond to the request. He was invited to a dinner at Quyuan Restaurant in

Nanjing by the Jiangsu Provincial Party secretary, Peng Chong.
He declined the invitation, deeply offending Peng. Under an
unclear set of circumstances, Tong Jun had for some time served
as a member of the Changzhou Political Consultative Conference,
but when a car arrived to take him to join the political activities,
he had refused to attend. From that time on, he received no
government benefits.

Many wondered why Tong Jun was not a member of the
Chinese Academy of Sciences. According to Tong Wen,[87] he had
once seen an application form for the academy on Tong Jun's desk,
but with nothing filled up.

Here is how Tong Jun evaluated his best friend and colleague
in his eulogy:

> Yang Tingbao was not only blessed with exceptional talent
> for design, but he was incorruptible, fair-minded, and
> scrupulous in all things; a gentle, scholarly gentleman of
> high moral standing.[88]

In a co-authored article, Zhao Chen and Tong Wen attempted
to answer why Tong Jun turned down Liang Sicheng's invitation to
come to Beijing, staying on in Nanjing instead.

> The reason Tong Jun ultimately chose to stay in Nanjing
> rather than accept a position in Beijing at Tsinghua
> University is something people have often discussed.
> He treasured his friendship with Liu Dunzhen and Yang
> Tingbao too much to be away from them, and there was
> a close-knit bond their three wives had formed. The deep
> affection among these three masters of the architecture
> sphere had become a salutary tale that spread widely in the
> field; one that moved a great many people.[89]

Tong Jun was, by nature, a very private, and not particularly
sociable, man. In Nanjing, his friendships with Yang Tingbao, Liu

Zhang Yongsen, Yang Tingbao, and Tong Jun on a site visit
tour in Yangzhou, China

Dunzhen, and Zhang Yuzhe gave him more comfort than anything
else in an unsettled life.

After returning to Nanjing from treatment in Beijing, the first
thing he did was take his son Tong Linsu to call on Yang Tingbao's
widow, Chen Faqing. Tong Linsu recalled:

> *The first thing Father did when came back to Nanjing*
> *was tell me to ride a rickshaw to take him to the homes of*
> *Uncles Yang Tingbao and Liu Dunzhen to visit their wives*

and pay respects as both Uncle Yang and Uncle Liu had passed away. Father's friendship with Uncle Yang was something special. When Father had surgery at Nanjing Regional Military General Hospital, my brother and I were at his side. When he heard that Uncle Yang had suddenly fallen ill and that his children were unable to rush home, he told one of us to go look after Uncle Yang. We both volunteered, so Father had my brother go. He spent the night in the hospital, not leaving until Uncle Yang's niece came to take his place.[90]

Even after his father died, Linsu and his wife continued to call on Yang Tingbao's and Liu Dunzhen's wives and families in Nanjing every Chinese New Year. The enduring close friendship among the three families is a rarity in academic circles.

Yang Tingbao, Tong Jun, and Chen Jing, Liu Dunzhen's wife

— CHAPTER FIVE —

Eyes Like a Camera

In 1981, two books—*Tong Jun Watercolor Album*[91] and *Tong Jun Sketch Album*[92]—were published. Most of the artwork was executed in 1930, when the author was touring Europe. Tong Jun's schoolmate and confidant Chen Zhi wrote:

Tong Jun studied oil painting as a child, which created a solid foundation for sketching. At Tsing Hua, he devoted much of his time to watercolors. At the University of Pennsylvania, he studied under the renowned American watercolor artist George W. Dawson, under whose mentorship he made great progress. His rapid brush strokes and deft touch on the paper had his fellow students saying, "He has eyes like a camera." He could work in pencil, charcoal, crayons, and chalk, as well as watercolors—in which he excelled, incorporating bold, vigorous strokes, brilliant colors, and multiple themes that had remarkable appeal. He was adept in employing fluid, broad brush strokes, as well as meticulously controlled sketches.[93]

From 1933 to 1937, Tong Jun studied traditional Chinese painting with artist Tang Dingzhi who was seeking refuge in Shanghai. Tang, also named Tang Di, was a Beijing-based master of calligraphy and painting. Twenty-two years older than Tong Jun, he was in the prime of his life when Tong Jun studied under

1930, Tong Jun on a steamship bound for Europe

him. Though he had established his name as a calligrapher and painter, his declaration of self was beyond those skills: "I am first, a physiognomist; second, a poet; third, a calligrapher; and fourth, a painter."[94]

"The two individuals were well matched in temperament—staunch and upright."[95] Though in later years Tong Jun was caught up in the war and drifting throughout much of China, he never let go of two of his teacher's paintings. Both, regrettably, were lost in house searches during the Cultural Revolution. Tong Jun's "towering mountains, deep valleys and hidden streams, sweeping dark lines and lively ink spots are enchanting."[96]

On June 12, 1978, Tong Jun painted a scene for his Tsing Hua College roommate, Lin Tongji.

He painted on a vertical scroll to emphasize the height, distance, and depth of the scene. A steep precipice occupies the center, bordered on the left by several mountain peaks and a waterfall cascading into a stream flowing through a valley. The closer scene is a hut under ancient pines, and within a bamboo grove, in front of which stand a pair of robed recluses, likely to represent the painter and his old friend.[97]

The colophon on that painting notes:

It always makes me emotional when I recall all my talented roommates and classmates from earlier days, who are now spread across all over the world and cannot easily meet again. When I visited Mount Huangshan (eastern China) and viewed Shixin Peak, I thought how wonderful it would be to build a hut at the foot, where I could feast on the sunrise and drink the dew, mock the moon, and sing with the wind. Close friends would stop by from time to time, knocking at my door to search for poetic expressions and

reminisce about the past. Would this not be great joy? My
old friend Tongji probably shared my sentiment, but might
laugh at my naivete, so I conveyed his feeling in this playful
work. Ten days before the Winter Solstice in the Dingsi
year, Tong Jun at midnight.[98]

Though he had laid aside his brush for years, this painting is testimony to his reputation as a fine painter of traditional Chinese art.

Tong Jun seldom showed his work. Only when friends like Yang Tingbao and Zhang Yuzhe dropped by and happened to mention them did he take some of his work out of a camphor chest; paintings that had managed to survive war and political movements. During the Cultural Revolution, teachers and students from the architecture department at Nanjing Institute of Technology searched his house and confiscated the camphor chest, tossing it onto the back of a three-wheeler. Du Shunbao, a member of the department, said, "That chest is too beat up to be of any use," and he took it out of the yellow croaker and dumped it on the ground, thereby saving the precious paintings from destruction.[99]

According to Yang Yongsheng (a publisher), sometime in the early 1980s, when artist Shao Yu saw Tong Jun's watercolors, he said: "I honestly did not know that there was anyone in China who could paint such fine watercolors. In my view, there are not many people in the country who could be this good."[100]

Nowhere in Tong Jun's watercolors will you find anything Chinese. They are purely the product of an overflowing passion for the West. Someone who knows nothing of Tong Jun's background will surely assume that the painter is an unpolished individual with long hair and a scraggly beard, down on his luck, smoking and drinking in excess, and probably the victim of a failed marriage; someone like Van Gogh, perhaps. As for his paintings, not many people are able to fully appreciate both their artistic excellence and their substance, for that takes a certain

Scenic painting by Tong Jun for Lin Tongji

Tong Jun and architect Wu Liangyong reviewing watercolor
paintings at Tong Jun's home

background and temperament. There are few who would have undergone similar training and the European experience that Tong Jun had enjoyed. Tong Jun gave a copy of his watercolor album to Wilma Fairbank, who had majored in art. She told him that her mother had taken her and her sisters to Europe that same year when Tong Jun had his grand tour in Europe. "If I were an art critic," she said, "I'd place Tong Jun's watercolors at the peak of Chinese artists, and would put him in a class by himself in the West for his technique and powerful sense of individuality—work that is nearly impossible to emulate."[101]

In the foreword to his published painting album, Tong Jun discussed architecture and travel:

> *If one is asked to observe and then understand the three features of architectural structures—line, surface, and form—one must draw what one sees to fortify the memory of what is seen. Time is usually of the essence, but if one is especially interested in the historical and cultural backgrounds of a particular place, and is moved by what one sees and the passage of time, while not being in a hurry, then watercolor paintings fit the bill better than most. Watercolors are very demanding. When painting outdoor scenes, before filling in the sketch, one must first envision a complete picture, and then make quick pencil strokes, starting with the sky, and arranging the shaded parts from top to bottom, as early, and as suitably as possible. Then, one can add muted architectural colors and highlights, but leave white spaces. That way, the basic contrast between light and dark is established. Each application of color is final, no going over, in order to retain its freshness and purity. Sometimes the color is applied to wet spots on the paper. Never, under any circumstances, use white chalk.[102]*

In regard to sketching, he wrote:

When traveling, a pencil is the most convenient and economical tool you have; it has the advantage of accessibility and an erase function; a pencil drawing can serve as a draft reminder or a record of sketches; it is ideal for detailed, time-consuming sketches, and sometimes produces excellent works.[103]

In his foreword, whether Tong Jun is discussing watercolors or sketches, he takes the opportunity to bring up Chinese history. A 1982 letter to his nephew, Tong Yan, gives a clear picture of how he interprets traditional Chinese art:

In today's world, many cultures are beginning to make contact, interact, and flow between one another. Not all Western artists need to understand Chinese painting, but Chinese who study art must study Chinese painting. That is because being Chinese precludes the possibility of not understanding one's own traditional art. Chinese painting incorporates philosophy and a harmonious merging of literature and nature, and is buttressed by a long tradition of theoretical analysis. The West has a long way to go to catch up.[104]

In his introduction to the 1995 edition of Tianjin Science & Technology Press's print of *Tong Jun Architectural Painting,*[105] Wu Liangyong wrote:

Back when we were still in school, Tong Jun's drawings topped those of the revered Western master Vignal, and even surpassed his work in his lofty conception. Tong Jun's watercolors possess important historical and urban aesthetic value.[106]

Painting occupied an extraordinary place in Tong Jun's mind. "In our downstairs drawing room," Tong Wen recalled, "Granddad

Tong Jun watercolor: Piazza San Marco in Venice

had me take the chest with his watercolors down for him to show Wu Liangyong. I turned them over, one at a time, as they made comments in Chinese and English. He said to Wu, 'Architecture has its merits, but painting is the real thing.'"[107]

Almost thirty years after Tong Jun's death, in 2012, Wang Shu quoted Tong Jun in his acceptance speech for the Pritzker Prize: "Architecture has its merits, but painting is the real thing."[108]

When Tong Jun was painting outdoor scene in the Nanjing suburbs in the 1950s, he was taken to the police precinct to be investigated for espionage. He stopped painting the outdoors after that. He more or less stopped painting altogether, but acted as advisor to his students. When he was at his peak, he abandoned the "real thing"—painting.

In his recollection of Tong Jun's extraordinary teaching qualities at Northeastern University, his student, Zhang Bo wrote:

Professor Tong possessed a unique set of skills. When a student's canvas surface was uneven or damaged by a scraping knife, he would personally lend a hand to save the painting. As he was accomplished in the basic skills of sketching and watercolors, he could usually give the damaged surface a new life through simple coloring and minor adjustments.[109]

Someone once revealed that Tong Jun had been invited to create a bird's-eye-view painting of the Northeastern University campus for the 1950 achievement exhibit at the anniversary celebration of the founding of the school. He started by having some of his students produce sketches of the major buildings, from which he created a bird's-eye overview with charcoal on a large poster board. He used simple, clean lines and confident strokes before applying white chalk on the spots where light shone; like painting the eyes on a dragon, creating an outstanding work through improvisation.

In 1959, in a competition on the bridgeheads of the Yangzi River Bridge in Nanjing, Tong Jun produced a colored performance graph on size No. 1 drawing paper, with muted colors of the stone bridgeheads on both banks, leaving the river itself completely white.

These two drawings, executed under pressure, were praised as models in the architecture department at Nanjing Institute of Technology, but also produced sighs over wasted potential.

To ensure that his European sketches would hold up permanently, before leaving for Europe, he purchased the finest paper and oils money could buy. Ten years later, when World War II broke out, German aircrafts indiscriminately bombed many of the sketched sites out of existence. For that reason, these paintings— which would survive the War of Resistance, the Chinese Civil War,

Tong Jun watercolor: Salzburg's Königssee

and the destruction of the Cultural Revolution— must be seen as being of inestimable value. After nine decades, the colors of the paintings remain vivid, so that generations of scholars can enjoy a bygone English countryside and the Norman style, and can see the classy elegance of England's institutes of higher learning.

In 2002, Tong Jun's family donated all his artwork to Southeast University (originally Central University, changed to Nanjing Institute of Technology, and, in 1988, changed back to Southeast University), where he had worked for nearly half a century. In 2016, Tong Jun's grandson, Tong Ming, designed the Tong Jun Studio at Southeast University.

In 2012, Southeast University Press published *Sienna—Tung Chuin Grand Tour Diaries*[110] and *Sienna—Tung Chuin Grand Tour Painting*,[111] compiled by Tong Ming. He named them Sienna, and reveals why:

> *Once, during a casual conversation, he remarked*
> *that sienna was his favorite color. We had no way of*
> *explaining his fondness for a particular color; maybe*
> *because it was the color of so many European brick*
> *buildings, which was a color which, under the sun's rays,*
> *displayed different shades of sienna. Like his personality:*
> *substantive and solid.*[112]

— CHAPTER SIX —

A Remembrance of Liang Sicheng for Wilma Fairbank

In 1980, Tong Jun began an extensive correspondence with Wilma Fairbank, writer and wife of John Fairbank, helping her publish posthumous work by Liang Sicheng, supplying her with firsthand material for her biographical work on Liang Sicheng and Lin Huiyin.

John King Fairbank was a tenured professor at Harvard University, a renowned historian and one of the best-known China watchers. A leading American authority in research in the field of modern and contemporary Chinese history, he founded Harvard University's Center for East Asian Research. He served as vice chairman of the American Far East Association, chairman of the Asia Society, chairman of the History Society, and chairman and leading member of the board of directors of East Asian Research. Fairbank first arrived in China with his wife, Wilma Fairbank in 1932, and worked as an instructor in economic history at Tsinghua University. He met Liang Sicheng and Lin Huiyin in Beijing in 1932, with whom he developed a deep and abiding friendship. When Liang toured the United States in 1947, Wilma Fairbank interviewed him when he stayed at her home. Years later, in 1979, with the thaw in Sino-American relations and the information exchange just getting underway, she returned to China to visit friends and former colleagues of Liang and Lin. The couple had passed away in 1955 and 1972, respectively.

Tong Jun's graduation photo from University of Pennsylvania

It is no exaggeration to say that John and Wilma Fairbank were Liang and Lin's most cherished friends. Not only did they help the struggling couple financially during World War II and use their influence to facilitate Liang and Lin's research, but they collected Liang's most important scholarly work, including hand-drawn maps and manuscripts from the time when he worked at the Society for Research in Chinese Architecture (SRCA). Wilma Fairbank spent a considerable amount of time and effort to have these valuable works published in the United States—as Liang had so wished—in 1995, long after Liang's death. She also wrote a joint biography of Liang and Lin, relating stories about their life and work. Without the Fairbanks, Liang and Lin's scholarly work and other contributions may well have been lost to history.

Wilma Fairbank's handwritten manuscript of the biography was primarily based on conversations at her home during Liang's 1946–1947 six-month stay in the United States, and events that occurred at his home in Beijing in the 1930s. Following the establishment of Sino-American relations, in the 1980s Fairbank made plans to publish Liang's collected essays and biography. Tong Jun, who was Liang's schoolmate at Tsing Hua College and dormmate at the University of Pennsylvania, along with Chen Zhi, helped her a great deal in this project, supplying her with material on Liang—his life, work, and family—from the 1920s through to the time of Liberation in 1949, and beyond. In a letter to Fairbank, Tong Jun told her about an essay[113] Liang had published in *Asia Magazine* in July 1941, on Foguang Temple (Shanxi Province). They discussed Liang's "Five Early Chinese Pagodas"[114] and his comprehensive, detailed reports on Anji and the Yuntong Bridges in Zhaozhou, Hebei. Tong Jun also made some corrections to her manuscript. Two months after he last saw her in Nanjing, Tong Jun underwent surgery for his recurring cancer; within half a year, he had passed away. Prior to that they had maintained a steady correspondence about her Liang Sicheng books for six months.

In "Tong Jun and Architectural Academy in Nanjing" ("Tong Jun Yu Nanjing De Jianzhu Xueshu Shiye," a co-authored article by Zhao Chen and Tong Wen), Zhao Chen and Tong Wen describe how Tong Jun and Liang Sicheng's friendship developed over the three periods during which they spent time together:

> *The first period—1921–1924—was when Liang was a student at Tsing Hua College, prior to leaving for the United States; the second period—1925–1928—was when they were both architecture students at the University of Pennsylvania studying under Professor Paul Philippe Cret; the final period—1930–1931—was when both were professors at Northeastern University.*[115]

In 1921, when Tong Jun began classes at Tsing Hua College, Liang Sicheng was already a very active "star pupil," engaged in a variety of activities. They shared art editing duties for Tsing Hua College's yearbook, which was a highly pleasant experience for them both, and also the catalyst for them to recognize each another's artistic talents. Especially during their three years as students studying overseas in the United States—where they were roommates—they were like brothers; away from home, with similar aspirations providing them with an uncommonly deep friendship.

People greatly admired Tong Jun's special talents. He and another exemplary student, Yang Tingbao, were considered the pride of the cohort of Chinese students. As a close friend, Liang was as clear as anyone could be regarding Tong Jun's knowledge of architecture and his attainments in the field. After Liang returned to China in 1928, his father, the celebrated Liang Qichao whose ability to maneuver social connections was unequalled, arranged for his son to join the faculty of Northeastern University in Shenyang, and assume the duties of chair of the Architecture Department. Naturally, Liang hoped that Tong Jun, who at the time was working for Ely Jacques Khan's architectural firm in

Liang Sicheng

97

New York, would return to help him establish this new field of academic study.

Liang Sicheng once made the following comment regarding Tong Jun's abilities: "His knowledge and administrative skills were ten times greater than mine."[116] In order to win Tong Jun over, Liang even offered him the chairmanship, which Tong politely declined. But in the end, he did not disappoint Liang.

In June, 1930, Tong Jun returned to Shenyang from the United States via Europe and accepted an invitation to join the Northeastern University Architecture Department faculty; a strong, fresh addition to this authentic "Chinese version" of the classic UPenn system. In 1931, Liang left Northeastern University for Beijing to take charge of the Society for Research in Chinese Architecture, and since their other friend from the university, Chen Zhi, had gone to Shanghai to run an architectural firm, Tong Jun assumed the chairmanship of the department to ensure its survival. Soon after, following the September 18 Japanese invasion (September 18 Incident), Northeastern University's students fled and, with the help of Tong Jun, were relocated—the 1930 class to Central University in Nanjing (later renamed Nanjing Institute of Technology), and the 1928 and 1929 classes to Shanghai, as students at The Great China University. He called upon architects in the city to offer free tutorials for two years, at the end of which the students received diplomas from Northeastern University. Over those two years, Tong Jun often paid for students' living and traveling expenses out of his own pocket, and when no classroom was available, he held classes and exams in his own home. After suffering untold educational hardships, the first class of Northeastern University's architecture students graduated and went out into the world and entered the job market.

Tong Shibai recalled:

Some Northeastern University students came to our apartment in Shanghai for classes. One day there were ten

1930, Faculty and students of Northeastern University
Architecture Department
(front row, left to right) Cai Fangyin, Tong Jun, unknown,
Chen Zhi, Liang Sicheng, and Zhang Gongfu

*of them. "Time to take an exam," I heard Father say. They
all found seats. Some sat at the dining table, others sat in
chairs next to tea tables, a few used the turntable bench
for a desk, and some even sat at the large desk Father and
I used. My job switched from bringing tea and water to
supplying paper, pencils, and erasers. The next morning, I
heard mother complain about all the pencil shavings on the
floor. Not long after that, they came to say good-bye, likely
after finding work upon graduation, and from then on, if
they happened to be in Shanghai over New Year's or other
holidays, or on business trips, they never failed to come
pay their respects to Father. Liu Hongdian, Guo Yulin, and
Liu Zhiping were frequent guests at the house.*[117]

When he learned that the first class of his hand-picked students from Northeastern University Architecture Department had graduated after all their trials and tribulations, how could Liang Sicheng not admire Tong Jun for the exemplary model he had established for them? In a letter to this first class, Liang was unambiguous in his praise, calling Tong Jun "a ray of light" during "a time of national crisis, when education had to be halted."[118]

Wilma Fairbank's letter to Tong Jun on April 25, 1982 asking for materials on Liang Sicheng for her biography triggered Tong Jun's recollection of Liang Sicheng:

> *I can also furnish you with an anecdote or two in his (and my) Phila. days, since we shared the same room, that might be of interest to you. It makes one sad to fondle souvenirs like last summer's roses and to revive memories that fade with the snows of yesteryear.*[119]

Tong Jun expressed his fondness for Liang Sicheng, his friend and schoolmate, at two institutions—as dormmate and as colleague—in unambiguous terms. He also praised him as a great scholar, just like his father, Liang Qichao, though he found him (Liang Sicheng) to be, politically, anything but astute, and deeply self-contradictory. His statement below is an example of this self-contradiction of Liang Sicheng—which he made after an incident in which Lin Huiyin's father was killed by a stray bullet in the northeast, evoking Liang Sicheng to vow that he would never again work for Manchurian warlords.[120]

"But I could never understand," he wrote, "why two years later he went to Mukden (Shenyang), to start the architecture school right under the nose of the general who caused the death of his own father-in-law."[121]

Wilma Fairbank had not realized that being hired in Northeastern University's Architecture Department changed the course of Tong Jun's life.

In 1928, after the warlord Zhang Zuolin was killed by a bomb at Huanggutun Railway Station (Liaoning Province, Shenyang), Liang Sicheng and Lin Huiyin established an architecture department at Northeastern University and began holding classes in the fall. The students were intellectually active. In December, during the regime change, they created a mocking slogan: "Congratulations to the Commander in Chief for his promotion to Vice Commander in Chief!"[122] By then, Chiang Kai-shek[123] had incorporated the troops of Zhang Xueliang, the army commander for Northeast China, sowing the seeds of a total occupation of Northeast China by the Japanese.

In 1930, when Tong Jun was studying in the United States and interning at Ely Jacques Khan's firm, and had reached the pinnacle, he received a telegram in New York from Liang Sicheng, inviting him to join the Northeastern University faculty. By that time, Tong Jun was a rising star in the realm of American architecture, winning the first medal award of the Arthur Spayd Brooke Prize and the Beaux-Arts Institute of Design Architectural Competition, out of contestants from forty institutions. This invitation from Liang promised the realization of a cherished dream: first, this was an opportunity to return home, to live among three generations of his family; second, reading and teaching were his passions; third, Northeast China was an area under development, opening up rich possibilities for architectural firms; and, fourth, the salary was nearly three times that at Tsinghua University (previously named Tsing Hua College) and Peking University, and the faculty was made up exclusively of his Tsing Hua College and UPenn schoolmates.

After receiving the appointment letter to Northeastern University, Tong Jun changed his European travel plan to pass through Asia Minor and return to China via India, traveling instead through Siberia to reach Shenyang in August of 1930. During the 1930–31 academic year, the architecture department

Liang Sicheng created for the university had reached its peak, with the rise of the junior class. That year, Liang, Chen Zhi, Tong Jun, and Cai Fangyin all showed up for a group photo; only Lin Huiyin, who had gone to Beijing for health reasons, was not there; Liang and Lin were also partners. Tong Jun taught Western architecture and architecture design to first-year students, emphasizing the proportional training in classical columns, requiring them to commit to memory the colonnade equation. Liang Sicheng, Chen Zhi, and Tong Jun duplicated the UPenn model for the Architecture Department at Northeastern University, replicating Professor Paul Philippe Cret's "atelier system." There was little difference in age between teachers and students, creating a lively atmosphere. When a deadline for their work approached, all teachers and students burned the midnight oil, everyone busy with tasks; Liang carried an alarm clock to monitor the time and make sure the students turned in their work on time.

The good times were, however, short-lived. Just two years after the Architecture Department at Northeastern University was created, Chen and Lin fell victim to the harsh Shenyang climate and developed lung ailments, and since Liang and Chen both had sons, remaining in the northeast did not seem feasible. On top of that, a significant incident had also taken place, involving an ancient bell tower on a road in Shenyang, to the young marshal and the residence of the top leader then, Zhang Xueliang. The Northeast Army was planning to tear down the cultural site where the bell tower was; Liang wanted to propose instead that a detour be created around the tower and sought an audience with Zhang as the son of Liang Qichao, so as to get permission to preserve the site. Zhang refused to meet with Liang and went ahead and had his troops take the tower down in a single night. Not a stone was spared. Liang Sicheng was livid and referred to Zhang as "warlord shit" in his belligerent ranting. In June, he resigned his position and went to Beijing to join the

Society for Research in Chinese Architecture while Chen went to Shanghai to join Zhao Shen in launching Zhao Shen & Chen Zhi Architecture Firm. Only Tong Jun and Cai Fangyin remained at Northeastern University.

With Liang's departure, Tong Jun took over the chairmanship. A mere three months later, the September 18 Incident erupted, with Japanese artillery demolishing the university. It so happened that not long after, in 1933, the Nazis shut down Walter Gropius' Bauhaus School, with renowned architect Ludwig Mies van der Rohe as its last head. During the chaos of war, Tong Jun was unyielding in his determination to keep the department running, so he held classes in the Chinese inland (non-SAR areas) until the students graduated.

Fate had arranged a bumpy future for Tong Jun, a vagabond existence that began with September 18. He had found it hard to live with the pain and suffering caused by the Japanese invasion. Once, when his wife, Guan Weiran, went out with their youngest son, Tong Linbi, they were chased by an armed Japanese soldier; she managed to make it home, but spent three days in a state of semi-consciousness, which eventually caused her a weakened heart. In 1956, she suffered a heart attack and died in an ambulance on her way to the hospital. This left a scar in Tong Jun's life.

A young teacher recalled:

> *On one occasion, when Tong Jun was an old man, a leading member of the Nanjing Institute of Technology Architecture Department brought representatives of a Japanese architecture association to see Tong Jun in the reference room. When the guests were introduced, the old man closed the book he was reading, stood up, and without a word, walked around the visitors and left. They all waited for him to return, until they were told he'd gone home.*[124]

It wasn't clear if the reason Tong Jun refused to take Tanaka Tan on as his graduate mentee was because he was Japanese; but there can be no doubt that the hatred born of the Japanese invasion of his homeland had burned into his heart. This is despite the publication of his book *Modern and Contemporary Japanese Architecture*[125] in 1983.

On June 6, 1949, Liang Sicheng sent Tong Jun an impassioned letter:

> *Lao Tong, congratulations on your liberation. Although I'm a few days earlier, I'm sending you congratulations as someone from the "established place." Tsinghua was liberated a month earlier than Beijing, and from the very first day, the discipline of the PLA soldiers has left a deep impression. Following all manner of association with the communists, and observing their broad-mindedness and practical, fact-based attitude has earned our enthusiastic support. This time, China has undergone a successful revolution.*[126]

In the final sentence of the letter Liang wrote: "The government can make all the arrangements for your trip to Beijing, and I look forward to an early reply. Huiyin joins me in sending you warmest regards. In friendship, Sicheng."

Lacking any relevant documentation, we cannot know what Tong Jun wrote in response, but from that time on, these two old friends were no longer in frequent communication. In 1955, however, Tong Jun made a special trip to a Beijing hospital to visit the gravely ill Lin Huiyin. In 1964, Liang wrote to Tong Jun to say: "I haven't been to Nanjing once since Liberation."[127]

In Tong Linsu's reflection on why Tong Jun stayed away from Beijing, it was supposed that it was because Liang Sicheng was there and he worked closely with politicians. Liang seemed too political for Tong Jun's taste. Tong Jun preferred to steer clear of

A REMEMBRANCE OF LIANG SICHENG FOR WILMA FAIRBANK

A letter from Liang Sicheng inviting Tong Jun to Tsinghua
University

105

politics and was determined to keep it so. Nanjing, far less political, was the place for him, and so he used the "excuse" that he had a home in Nanjing and had no interest in interrupting his peaceful life, and hence wanted to remain there. Also, his long-time friends Yang Tingbao, Liu Dunzhen, Zhao Shen, and Chen Zhi, all, encouraged him to stay put and maintain their close relationship with each other.

In a September 1982 letter to Tong Jun, Wilma Fairbank wrote:

It is too bad that again my visit in Nanking was so brief. But I am grateful that the Liangs have brought us together, even these many years after they have been gone. And I count you as a real friend.[128]

Liang Sicheng (right) with colleagues

— CHAPTER SEVEN —

Are You Still Alive?

After 1950, Tong Jun dropped out of sight and was holed up in his house at 52 Wenchang Lane with his mounds of books, avoiding contact with the outside world. Meanwhile, in Hong Kong and Taiwan, he was highly respected. Books from mainland China were banned in Taiwan, with four exceptions, and those were widely distributed photocopied versions. One of those was Tong Jun's *Jiangnan Yuanlin Zhi (On Classical Gardens in Southeastern China)*.

As China began re-establishing relations with the outside in the late 1970s, Tong Jun one day received a query forwarded from Hong Kong: "Are you still alive?"[129] So many intellectuals had been tortured to death, and rumors that he had died during the Cultural Revolution had spread outside mainland China, leading to a full-page obituary in the Hong Kong *Ta Kung Pao* newspaper. The friend who had sent the query had not only made a special trip to Nanjing to see that he was still alive and well, but had even had a picture taken with him as proof.[130] To make an even more convincing case, Tong Jun also had a photo of him and his two grandsons taken in his yard. There is the hint of a smile on his face in this photo. Tong Wen wore a confused look, and Tong Ming looked unhappy and fidgety, as if he'd been forced to stop playing for the photo and couldn't wait to get back to having fun.

After this, Tong Jun started reaching out to people who had been making the same inquiry. From responses to his letters, he

Tong Jun with Tong Wen and Tong Ming in the yard of their
home at 52 Wenchang Lane

learned that many of his old friends had just been released from
incarceration; one of them, an old man from the northeast, had
spent the years in his prime locked up. Some of these friends
assured him that they had enough to get by and asked him to not
send any more money. Another said he hadn't seen any vegetables
in months. More than a few had died during one campaign or
another and were now in a different world.

Tong Jun received a newspaper clipping announcing a belated memorial for his schoolmate Wang Zaoshi. Wang had been a student leader at Tsing Hua College—one of the well-known "Three Anfu Stars of Tsing Hua," along with Luo Longji and Peng Wenying. He had gone to study in the United States in 1925, where he had earned his bachelor's, master's, and doctoral degrees at the University of Wisconsin. He entered the London School of Economics as a researcher in 1929, returning to China the next year to take up duties as Dean of Arts and Letters and the chair of the Political Science Department at Shanghai's Kwang Hua University. Wang wielded substantial influence as a patriotic-democratic individual. In November 1936, along with Shen Junru, Zhang Naiqi, Zou Taofen, Li Gongpu, Sha Qianli, and Shi Liang, he was arrested in what was later known as the "Seven Gentlemen Incident."[131] After Liberation in 1949, Wang served as a member of the North China Military and Political Affairs Committee, a member of the Standing Committee of the Shanghai Municipal Political Consultative Conference, a professor at Fudan University's Political Science and History Departments (in Shanghai), and chair of the Modern History Teaching and Research Group at Fudan. He was labeled a "Rightist" in 1957 by CPC. His speeches at the Chinese People's Political Consultative Conference, including "My Views and Recommendations Concerning China's Democratic and Legal System" and "My View of Bureaucratism" were collected in the publication *Excerpts of Rightist Wang Zaoshi's Viewpoints*,[132] subjecting him to virulent criticism. During the Cultural Revolution, he was tortured at the Shanghai No. 1 Prison (Shanghai Diyi Kanshousuo). He died on August 5, 1971. His four children suffered collateral consequences and all followed him in death. The wrongs he suffered were righted in May 1980, and on August 20, a memorial was jointly held for him by the Shanghai Consultative Conference and Fudan University.

Tong Jun's devoted friend Peng Wenying had also died some twenty years before. Peng was the highest scoring Jiangxi Province enrolee at Tsing Hua College in 1917. In 1927 he received a Bachelor of Arts in Political Science from the University of Wisconsin and, a year later, a Master of Arts in Political Science from Columbia University. He once helped Zhou Enlai[133] escape danger when he was engaged in underground work in Shanghai. In the wake of the "Seven Gentlemen Incident," he was involved in rescue work under Song Qingling (second wife of Chinese revolutionary leader Sun Yat-sen). On the eve of Liberation in 1949, the chief of Nanjing, Shanghai & Hangzhou Garrison Command, Tang Enbo, issued a command: "Stop at nothing to arrest Shi Liang and Peng Wenying."[134] Peng hid out until Liberation, after which he was elected member of the Democratic League of China, vice-chairman of the Shanghai Democratic League, and a member of the North China Military and Political Affairs Committee. He was labeled a "Rightist" in 1957 and forced to give up all his official posts though he refused to admit to any wrongdoing, even writing a letter to Mao Zedong. He died of illness in 1962, following his wife and son, who had suffered because of him. During the Cultural Revolution, all three family grave sites were desecrated out of existence. In Mao Zedong's essay "Beat Back the Attacks of the Bourgeois Rightists,"[135] he specifically listed Peng Wenying as a target. Zhang Chunqiao,[136] under the pseudonym Chang Shu, wrote an article entitled "Call Peng Wenying to Account."[137] Peng was one of the five "Rightists" who received no redress after the Cultural Revolution.

Tong Jun was surprised and elated to learn that his Tsing Hua College schoolmate, Sun Dayu, who was also criticized by name by Mao Zedong, was still alive.

Sun, a Yale graduate, returned to China in the early 1930s to assume professorial positions at Peking, Zhejiang, Jinan, and Fudan Universities. As a member of the renowned literary

Tong Jun's Tsing Hua College schoolmate Sun Dayu

Crescent Society, he published poetry collections and devoted considerable time and energy to the study and translation of Shakespeare. Within academic circles, there was a jovial acknowledgment that there were only one and a half Shakespeare experts: Sun Dayu was one, and everyone else combined to make a half.

Tong Jun with Tsing Hua College United States overseas schoolmates

In "Beat Back the Attacks of the Bourgeois Rightists," Mao Zedong wrote:

If obstinate men like Sun Dayu refuse to make the change, so be it. We have a lot to do now. It would be impossible to keep on hitting out at these types, day in day out, for the next fifty years! There are people who refuse to correct their mistakes, and they can take them into their coffins when they go to see the King of Hell.[138]

Sun was an incorruptible man, and as a result, was subjected to frequent criticism after Liberation. In the anti-Rightist campaign,[139] he angrily accused several leaders in Shanghai of being counter-revolutionaries. After being "named" by Mao Zedong, he was also labeled an ultra-Rightist in 1957, at the conclusion of the anti-Rightist campaign; then, on June 2, 1958, he was accused of slander and false accusations by the Shanghai Municipal Intermediate People's Court and sentenced to six years in prison as one of the two most influential Rightists to receive a judicial finding of guilt. After his release from prison, he was dragged up onto a stage to be struggled against Cultural Revolution Red Guards. He fought back with his fists, was labeled an active counter-revolutionary, and locked up in Shanghai Tilanqiao Prison for another two years. He was a special individual there, thanks to his unique personality; and despite being skin and bones, he vigorously defended himself, unyielding to the end, crunching chicken bones for nourishment, slurping piping-hot, thin porridge fearlessly, surviving under terrible conditions, until he was inexplicably released.

Tong Jun and Sun Dayu had been out of touch for more than twenty years. When Tong Jun learned that Sun Dayu had survived unimaginable horrors and was living in a shack in Shanghai's Hongkou District, he immediately sent his son, Tong Linsu, from Nanjing to Shanghai to see his friend. Sun was living in abominable conditions, forced to catch rain in buckets, owing to a leaky roof. "Confined to crude lodgings and awaiting government redress," Sun was worried, not about the refusal of his one-time workplace, Fudan University, to accept him back, but "over the total destruction of the remnants of a pitiful educational policy and institutions dating back to the Opium Wars—the restoration of which presented a formidable challenge."[140]

While re-examination and rectification regarding "Rightists" proceeded throughout the country, Sun Dayu's case, like those of Zhang Bojun,[141] Luo Longji, Peng Wenying, Chu Anping,[142] and Chen Renbing,[143] was not rectified, serving to prove that the political campaign against the intelligentsia and beyond was absolutely correct and that he was yet another necessary sacrificial lamb. Fortunately for him, East China Normal University in Shanghai hired him as a second-tier professor after his release. Having reached old age by then, he was mainly involved in research. Sun's Tilanqiao Prison mate, Yan Zuyou,[144] noted:

> *Year in and year out, Sun Dayu slept during the day and spent the whole night writing, leaving a prolific corpus of work. He devoted the last twenty years of his life to translating into English thousands of years of Chinese poetry, from Han and Wei Music Bureau ballads to songs of Chu, as well as poems by Tang and Song poets, employing the classic British sonnet rhyming scheme. He also translated into Chinese Shakespearean plays, sticking to the fourteen-line sonnet structure as best he could. "I'm the only one who can do this," he has been quoted as saying, "because of my familiarity with both the sonnet and with the metrics of classical Chinese verse." I doubt that there is another person in China or England who can do that.*[145]

Sun Dayu's "Rightist" label was not removed until 1984.

Another of Tong Jun's Tsing Hua College schoolmates, Xu Jian, who studied at Cornell University (New York) and Massachusetts Institute of Technology (MIT) revealed that he was suffering from reactive paranoia, which affected his brain. In his letters to Tong Jun, he avoided giving details of his suffering during the Cultural Revolution, but did describe in detail how other schoolmates were getting along, including Wang Shizhuo.

Wang Shizhuo wrote to tell Tong Jun that he had enjoyed a meteoric rise by being classified as a worker. Wang, who held a master's degree from MIT, was a pioneer in China's aviation industry. As a major force in the development of aviation in China, he presided over the design and construction of China's first wind tunnel and also participated in the training of scholars in aviation research, together with Qian Xuesen (a fellow student), as a foremost figure, making major contributions to the early development of the aviation industry. After being toppled, he changed one of the characters in his name to represent "rebirth." The redressing of Wang's case took a more circuitous route. First, he planned an appeal for justice to Qian Xuesen, who occupied a high position in the central government at that time, but received no response from Qian, so he sought out another Tsing Hua College schoolmate, Gao Shiqi.

At that time, Gao Shiqi was a renowned popular science writer who had studied at the University of Wisconsin and the University of Chicago. To his misfortune, during an experiment, he contracted viral encephalitis, which slowly led to near total paralysis. In the decades to follow, though "the devilish disease confined him to a chair,"[146] he managed to contribute more than a million words of unparalleled popular science writing to his readers. After returning to China in 1930, Gao worked in Nanjing's Regional Central Hospital, but quit in anger over its evil practices and corruption, and devoted his time to writing and translating. When he published his first popular science piece in 1933,[147] he changed the characters

Wang Shizhuo

in his name to alter their meaning, professing his repugnance toward officialdom and greed. Gao suggested that Wang forward all his material to Hu Yaobang.[148] Barely able to speak, Gao wrote the request with his good, right hand. Hu forwarded Wang's request for redress to the Organization Department of the Communist Party with an order that their decision be returned to him. After Beijing and Nanchang (Jiangxi Province) passed the buck back and forth several times, the Nanchang Petroleum and Chemical Factory, where Wang had been sent for re-education through labor, restored his salary as an engineer, and the Nanchang School of Aviation reinstated his pre-1956 salary. Then the Organization Department and the United Front Department jointly assigned him to the Consultancy to the State Council.

When news of the fall of the Gang of Four[149] began making rounds, Tong Jun was not shocked and excited. He just went quiet. It seemed to him to be little more than a dim chapter in a very long, dark history, though he also sensed that it was a turning point in that history. So, he picked up his pen and began a fierce period of writing.

"I often noticed Father heading to his study after eight at night, not turning out the lamp until two in the morning," Tong Linsu said. "Sometimes the light would only be off for a short time."[150]

In 1976, after the announcement of the fall of the Gang of Four, Tong Jun's roommate at Tsing Hua College, Lin Tongji, came to see him in Nanjing. It was their first meeting since 1949. Lin, a renowned historian, translator, and Shakespearean scholar, graduated from the University of Michigan and earned a master's and doctoral degree in political science from the University of California at Berkeley, where he later taught in the Department of East Asian Languages. He returned home in 1934 to teach at Tianjin's Nankai University. After Liberation, he taught in the Department of Foreign Languages at Shanghai's Fudan University. Lin was labeled a Rightist in 1958 and suffered in the

Wang Shizhuo, Xu Jian, Gao Shiqi, and Tang Peisong

Cultural Revolution, and he was locked up for two years. Prior to Liberation, he and Tong Jun were two of the twenty-six special contributors to the magazine *Zhanguo Ce*. After 1949, though one worked in Nanjing and the other in Shanghai—where Lin's mouth got him into trouble and made his life difficult—Tong Jun never broke off relations with him, even sending him a copy of his latest work, *Jiangnan Yuanlin Zhi* in 1964.

Tong Wen recalls that at the time his grandfather greeted this old friend with an embrace, even though Lin's unjust accusation had not yet been redressed. After they sat down, with great emotion he intoned:

"You can fool all the people some of the time, and some of the people all the time, but you cannot fool all the people all the time."[151]

Tong Jun in the United States with his former schoolmates at Tsing Hua College (Xu Jian, second from left)

— CHAPTER EIGHT —

A Reunion of Three Brothers

In 1972, Tong Jun's younger brother, Tong Yin, sought refuge in Nanjing and stayed with them for more than two years. An overseas student in Japan, he was chief engineer for the Northeast Power Company for nearly fifty years. From the 1920s to the 1960s, he designed and led the construction of the power grid for the three northeast provinces. After going their own way in the wake of the September 18 Incident, the brothers managed to survive various disasters. A Leica camera in hand and decades-old American hiking boots on his feet, Tong Jun traveled with Tong Yin from Nanjing to She County in Anhui Province, where they climbed Huangshan's Tiandu peak. From there, they went to Shanghai for a reunion with their third brother, Tong Cun. That same year, Tong Jun visited Nanjing city's Zhan Garden—one of the treasures of Jiangnan (Suzhou) gardens—for the last time; it is not hard to imagine the depth of emotion he felt then.

Tong Jun's father, Enge, was the first member of the extended family to go to school. As a student from Fengtian Prefecture, he participated in the imperial examination, and was one of eleven candidates awarded a *jinshi* degree at the grade seven officer level. His influence on Tong Jun was extensive.

According to Tong Cun, because their mother—a Han Chinese from Shandong—migrated to Manchuria, Tong Jun, Tong Yin, and Tong Cun were considered to be of Manchu-Han mixed blood. After passing the imperial examination,[152] Enge established

Young Tong Jun and his father Enge in Shenyang's Haoran
neighborhood

a girls' normal school in Shenyang and served as its principal.
Using the authority of his position, he chose the top three girls—
all members of the Manchu Yellow Banner royal family—to be
his sons' wives. This was because his second—and favorite son—
Tong Yin, who was the 400- and 800-meter race champion of the
three northeast provinces, was friendly with one Miss Wang, the
girls' 400-meter champion. Their private romance had shocked
Enge, forcing him to decide upon arranged marriages for all three
sons. Tong Jun was married at nineteen, to Guan Weiran, née Guan
Suwen. After they were married, she worked as an elementary
school teacher. Most of warlord Zhang Zuolin's children were
her students, including Zhang Xuesi. The name of Tong Jun's
grandson, Tong Wen, is borrowed from his grandmother's maiden
name, while the name of his granddaughter, Tong Wei, is borrowed
from her grandmother's married name—both names so chosen to
memorialize his deceased wife.

Not long after becoming principal, Enge became the head of the Fengtian Education Office, the equivalent of an education bureau for the three northeast provinces. It was a job for which he was eminently qualified, since he had gained considerable experience by planning his sons' education. At the age of eight, Tong Jun was sent to Fengtian Kindergarten in Shenyang, where he was tutored by a Japanese lady. She taught him handicrafts, such as paper cutting, collaging, and wood carving. Once, while carving a model train, he cut his finger, which left a scar. At ten, he entered the Fengtian No. 1 Elementary School, where his father insisted that he be taught the Chinese classics, committing to memory texts he did not understand. Seven years of memorizing the classics established a fine foundation in classical Chinese and planted the seed of the writing style that he would use later in life. At seventeen, Tong Jun entered Fengtian Number One Middle School, where he received a broad-based, modern education. During this time, he often went to the local YMCA (Young Men's Christian Association) to attend lectures on science and the arts given primarily by returned teachers from Japan. Lectures on world geography and history opened windows to other civilizations for the young Tong Jun. He began a diligent self-program of English study, reading a Shanghai English-language newspaper after class and making frequent visits to the YMCA for lectures in English. He also began studying Western oil painting and pencil sketches. A hundred years later, we can only marvel at Enge's plan and the foresight he showed toward his sons' education.

The day after the incident on September 18, 1931, Japanese troops occupied Shenyang and shut down the Beiling District campus of Northeastern University, forcing the dismissal of all the students. The streets were taken over by Japanese police, so Tong Jun and Guan Weiran moved their family from university housing to Enge's large compound in Haoran neighborhood. Chaos reigned in town as Korean thugs spread fear. On the third

Tong Cun as a student at Peking Union Medical College in
Beijing

day of the occupation, these Korean thugs broke into the Tong family compound and wrought havoc until they were stopped by Japanese-speaking Tong Yin. The family made plans to leave Japanese-controlled Shenyang and take refuge in Beiping (known today as Beijing).

On the fourth day, Tong Jun organized the move of thirty of the students of Northeastern University Architecture Department students to the south of the Great Wall, giving them traveling money from his own salary. He asked a German friend in Shenyang to contact the Japanese for permission to remove, from the sealed campus, plaster figures and the 400 slides that accompanied a copy of Sir Banister Fletcher's famous *A History of Architecture on the Comparative Method*,[153] which Liang Sicheng had bought in England. That evening, the whole family fled to Beiping. Tong Jun, his wife, father, Tong Yin's wife, and Tong Cun's wife (Tong Cun was studying at the Union Hospital in Beijing), together with their lightly packed luggage, boarded a train out. Tong Yin followed them a few days later, responsible for moving family property and furniture that filled a carriage. As the train approached the narrow pass at Shanhaiguan,[154] they came under attack by bandits who forced the train to stop. The train's armed guards returned fire, and when the conductor was killed in the gunfight, Tong Yin rushed up to the front from the rear, took control of the engine, and drove them out of danger. Many of Tong Jun's oil paintings and all of the 400 slides of Sir Fletcher's book were on that train. During the war years that followed, Tong Jun took those slides from Beijing to Shanghai, to Nanjing, and to Chongqing—four separate destinations—traveling thousands of miles. They were never out of his sight. Once the War of Resistance was won and a new China was proclaimed, the reopened Northeastern University was renamed Northeast Technical College; the Department of Architecture recruited students, and Tong Jun handed the slides, at no cost at all, to the college president, Zhang Liwu, saying simply,

Tong Jun in his later years with Tong Cun at 52 Wenchang Lane

but earnestly: "I carried them with me for twenty years, over thousands of miles. Now they're back home, where they belong."[155]

Not long after the family had made it to Beiping, Tong Jun received a letter from Chen Zhi inviting him to come to Shanghai in November and join him and Zhao Shen in their architecture firm; the firm's name had been changed to The Allied Architects (from Zhao Shen & Chen Zhi Architecture Firm). From then on, the three brothers each went their own way, not to be reunited again in Nanjing for forty years.

When a full-scale war broke out in 1937, Enge returned to Shenyang to live with his second son. He was by then in the twilight of his life and beyond medical help. He died in Shenyang, of a stroke, in 1945. During their father's last years, Tong Jun and Tong Cun were too far away to carry out their filial responsibilities. Tong Jun was in Guiyang and Tong Cun was in the United States, so neither was able to make the funeral arrangements, leaving the task to Tong Yin. Tong Cun did not even receive word that his father had died until spring 1945. Tong Jun supported his stepmother for the rest of her life.

Enge passed on his final instructions on his deathbed, but with the three brothers living apart, it was not until Tong Yin took refuge in Nanjing during the Cultural Revolution that they were reunited and he could pass these instructions on to his brothers. Their father had insisted that his descendants refuse to join any political party or the military, avoid the use of opium, not smoke, not gamble, be independent, live economically, and not seek quick riches.

Tong Cun was already a member of the Communist Party, but Tong Jun was able to adhere to all seven strictures. At the time when the three brothers learned of their father's instructions, they were facing a surge of revolutionary zeal and none of them knew what the future held for them. The first two items, especially, stood in direct opposition to the political climate, and it was anything but clear that they could follow his instructions, even within the family.

In fact, there were already Chinese Communist Party members and People's Liberation Army members among Tong Jun's sons.

As the eldest son, Tong Jun assumed his family responsibilities in a very traditional manner. When he learned that the ancestral graves had been desecrated during the Cultural Revolution, he knelt for a long time before his father's photograph and, feeling great resentment and bitterness, said to his grandson Tong Wen, "It makes a person roll over in his grave."[156] The Tong family had scrupulously maintained a family history that was subjected to careful research and diligent editing. The original Han Chinese name of the clan was Lang—part of the Manchu Blue Banner. Tong Linsu recalled that on all major holidays, his father would perform all the rites of respect to his own father and demanded of his sons that they do the same.[157] Enge was a strict disciplinarian who trained his son to be cautious and steady in all things. Tong Yin, on the other hand, had an outgoing personality, enjoying the company of others. He often took Tong Wen out to buy electronic components and helped him make circuit boards. As for Tong Cun, his fondness for research and his creative achievements made an especially powerful impression on Tong Wen.

Soon after Tong Yin returned to the northeast from Nanjing, he died tragically in 1977, in privation, impoverished by political circumstances. As for Tong Cun, despite his many incomparable contributions to the country in research on antibiotics, and the special treatment he enjoyed from the government, he was attacked as the Cultural Revolution deepened; what was even more tragic was that his wife was detained and struggled against, and forced to write self-criticisms (forced "confessions") which destroyed her mental equilibrium; Tong Cun had been a loyal member of the Communist Party. For an extended period of time, he kept a little of his salary for his family, but applied the bulk of his salary to Party dues. In his old age, he lived very simply, saving everything he could for his wife's future expenses, including medical costs.

The two brothers had been powerless to do anything about Tong Yin's miserable existence in the northeast, except to offer comforting words. Tong Jun did not attend his brother's funeral; he was depressed for a long time after Tong Yin's death.

In the disclosure material Tong Jun submitted in the 1960s, he wrote:

I am the oldest brother; my [first] brother Tong Zhongshu [Tong Yin] studied electric power engineering in Japan, returning to China in 1928, to work at the Shenyang Electric Power Grid Corporation. He then worked at a munitions factory. Later, he worked at the Northeast Power Administration, where, since Liberation, he still works. My younger sister-in-law, Yuzhi, is a housewife. My [second] brother, Tong Cun, graduated from the Beijing Union Medical College in 1932 and stayed on at the hospital as doctor of internal medicine. The hospital sent him to the

Tong Jun and Tong Yin in their later years at 52 Wenchang Lane

United States to study. He returned in 1946 and went to work at the Tiantan Central Epidemic Prevention Station in Beijing. In 1948, he was transferred to the Epidemic Prevention Station in Shanghai. After Liberation, he went to work at a pharmaceutical factory until he was sent to a medical research institute, where he works today. My [second] sister-in-law, Zhao Ruilin, is a housewife. My second brother was labeled a Rightist, the one stain on our family. The label was later removed.[158]

Tong Yin and his family

— CHAPTER NINE —

Under the Scorching Sun

In November 1960, an Architecture Design Institute was established at the Nanjing Institute of Technology, with Tong Jun as its first director. During the 1960s, he directed Western architecture research, and even though his research was not in line with the current political climate, he single-handedly embarked on untiring projects, such as Western gardens, the universal space by Ludwig Mies van der Rohe, the history of Parisian urban planning, and much more. At the same time, he put his hand to systematic research on Western modern architectural theories, spending decades in the reference room of the Nanjing Institute of Technology Architecture Department, reading extensively and researching diligently, carrying on pioneering work on Chinese modern architectural theory. In 1963, he was diagnosed with bladder cancer.

His brother Tong Cun scheduled and undertook his surgical treatment. The operation was a success and Tong Jun's recovery and return to research was swift.

In his Cultural Revolution self-criticism, he wrote:

In the fall of 1963, after the establishment of the third research lab in my department, as one of three "stinking intellectuals," I was given a work assignment. But then in November, I was admitted to the hospital, where I was operated on. I did not return to the college until May.

Tong Jun in his later years with Liu Guanghua

I took the next academic year off, returning to my research lab in September 1965. The Great Proletarian Cultural Revolution[159] was launched in the summer of 1966, and my lab was shut down. During that period, not counting the time I spent dealing with health issues and taking time off, I spent no more than a year and a half working there, and even then, I wasn't working full-time, coming in only on days when I felt like it, and not when I didn't. Instead, during my time off, I went to the reading room to scan journals and make my rounds to present a bad example, spreading the poison of my "scholarly attitude" among students and young faculty members.

Ninety percent of the foreign books that filled my bookcases came from America, England, with the remainder being

from France. Those foreign books meant a great deal to
me, obviously, but it was the recent English and American
capitalist offerings that were closest to my heart; especially
new ones from America, England, with the remainder being
from France. To be sure, there were plenty of publications
from socialist countries, but I only turned to publications
from the Soviet when I ran out of capitalist journals to
read, and also opened the occasional Polish or Hungarian
journals to leaf through when I was bored. After that, and
only then, did I flip through the recent Chinese journals that
lay around. There you have my priorities, and the order of
importance in my reading.[160]

During the Cultural Revolution, Tong Jun was mostly occupied with writing reports of his thinking and fulfilling demands by the Party and government to submit self-criticisms. Critics put forward by his colleagues reveal that the atmosphere in Nanjing was less heated than that in Beijing.

Zhang Zhizhong (his schoolmate from Tsing Hua College) commented on Tong Jun: "Although Yang Tingbao and Tong Jun were educated under the capitalist system stressing civilian use, after twenty or thirty years of work experience, they were able to deal with matters involving city planning and industrial construction."

Tong Jun responded: "I have formed no indelible bias toward specialization, and if that is the wave of the future, I hereby abandon the conservative approach and agree wholeheartedly."

Zhong Xunzheng commented:

Tong Jun is a very knowledgeable man of wide experience.
But when correcting designs, he focuses on the seeds and
throws away the melon, that is, placing the secondary over
the primary, which can lead to self-contradictions. I fervently
wish that Tong Jun would look at the overall design.

Tong Jun responded:

Sloppy corrections on design are an old failing of mine. I thought there were problems the students could solve on their own, but then realized that they did not, and needed make-up lessons. This does not serve them well, so I have resolved to give more thought to the students' level and make more detailed corrections.

Zhang Zhizhong further commented:

Tong Jun likes to joke around and split hairs, but he cares little for politics, comparing Rightists to children who steal a stool, saying that intellectuals have participated in manual labor since olden times. Unable to differentiate between feudalism, capitalism, and socialism, he must quickly leap forward!

Deng Siling commented:

He chats and laughs most of the time, and favors metaphors during discussions, but what he says lacks a political stance, and he is careless in correcting design drafts.

Tong Jun responded to his young colleagues Zhang Zhizhong, Zhong Xunzheng, and Deng Siling:

Caring little for politics and splitting hairs are major flaws of mine, a troublesome vestige of my capitalist background. I am firmly committed to criticizing these vestiges in my thinking and struggle to catch up with the times.

Students in the Architecture Department also weighed in: "Famous out in the world, no visible shadows on campus—Tong Jun and Yang Tingbao, our two professors."

Tong Jun responded:

*No visible shadow on campus was a student's criticism of me,
and I accept it. I will work hard to make my 'shadow' more
'visible,' but this 'shadow' can come out only in the sunlight
and will be absent at night, since I don't care to go out at night
(I don't see well in the dark and I go to bed early).*[161]

During the early days of the Cultural Revolution, the "cow
demons and snake-spirits"[162] were forced to memorize Mao
Zedong's Three Old Articles.[163] Tong Jun recited them with style.
He could recite them fluently, beginning with just about any
phrase, delivering it more smoothly and more adroitly than a monk
intoning scripture. When performing the Loyalty Dance,[164] he was
methodical to a fault, totally focused, as if all by himself; and with
not the slightest hint of a smile.

In 1966, when the Cultural Revolution was launched, Tong
Jun was stripped of all opportunities to teach and do research. His
grandson, Tong Ming, was born in 1968, but that event brought no
joy to the family, for that was the year in which Tong Jun's situation
turned ugly. His home was raided several times, he was subjected
to many struggle sessions, and he was forced to kneel time and
again. His new job at the college was as a janitor, sweeping floors
and cleaning toilets. He was also sent to Nanjing's Changjiang
Bridge construction site to break up rocks.

As shown in his record:

*October 15, 1968, a working day: At 8:30 in the morning, I
was sent to clean the Shatangyuan student dormitory, and
from there, to clean all the hallway toilets in the college. Then
from 2:30 to 5:30, I was sent to clean the Shatangyuan student
dormitory, and from there, to clean all the hallway toilets. I
then went to the area outside a room at the northwest corner
of the library to dig a hole and carry off the mud.*[165]

Most of what he wrote during this period was in the form of forced confessions, including his family situation and social ties before Liberation, his personal history before Liberation, his personal history since Liberation, his major flaws before Liberation, his reactionary opinions, a list of organizations he belonged to before Liberation, a list of construction designs he participated in, a list of what he wrote before Liberation, and what he still had to add in terms of social ties and social organizations.

Tong Jun's home in Wenchang Lane was repeatedly searched. "They came more than three times," Tong Wen wrote.

I was home each time, and I recall them as if they were there just yesterday. On one occasion, our nanny dragged me into the kitchen to stay out of the way. Another time, Grandfather held my hand to keep me from upsetting the Red Guards and making things worse. On yet another occasion, I chased their three-wheeler out to the Wenchang Lane entrance. The worst search was undertaken by the Red Guards who used to be from the same department as Tong Linsu. It was a true ransacking that turned the place upside down. What really got their attention were all of Grandma's Western tableware and Chinese dresses. One time, Qi Kang said that a female Red Guard named Zhu had walked off with a gold medal Grandfather had won at UPenn and he told me to go after her. Zhu's classmates also walked off with three or four of Grandfather's color renderings of the designs from his days at UPenn. He had never shown them to anyone except Qi Kang and Pan Guxi, who had been Grandfather's students, and who had been to our house once; Qi Kang said that Grandfather's talent was unmatched. Grandfather bravely kept a stern watch while they were searched and demanded that they write out a receipt for what they took. After his death, I found several

such receipts in a mahogany chest in his bedroom; one was
signed by Zhu. Even more shameful was how some people
also wrote receipts for how much cash they confiscated.[166]

It came to light that the Red Guard whom Qi Kang referred
to as Zhu was Zhu Guangfeng, a girl who had once slapped him so
hard it has permanently damaged his hearing in one ear.

When the Red Guards were searching Tong Jun's house, he
usually sat quietly to the side reading a book, as if it had nothing to
do with him. Once, when the Red Guards could find nothing more,
they summoned him to answer questions. He had them follow him
outside, where he pointed to a spot under a tree. As the Red Guards
dug out items, the family was shocked to observe that he had
buried his wife Guan Weiran's jewelry in that spot. None of it ever
found its way back.

Tong Linsu's and Tong Wen's narrations of their experiences
reveal that the house was searched eleven times, and most of the
searchers were either students of Tong Jun from the Architecture
Department of Nanjing Institute of Technology or Tong Linsu's
students and his colleagues from his Electronics Engineering
Department. Once, the child of one of his old friends had been
home when it was searched and his father was subjected to a
struggle session; he then brought people to Nanjing to search Tong
Jun's house.

Tong Linsu shared:

Father spoke little during the Cultural Revolution,
sometimes going all day without saying a word, at other
times just intoning classical poems. He was the same as
always at the table, sometimes getting up to check a word
in Webster's Dictionary, and then coming back to finish
his meal. One day, the rebels from the college showed up
to search the house, looking for anything belonging to the
"four olds."[167] *They gathered up phonograph records of*

*classical music and some old books, and loaded them up
on a three-wheeler. They then made Father wear a dunce's
cap and marched him down the street to deliver the "feudal,
bourgeois, reactionary" items to the school. Father was
an old man by then, so I took his place out on the street,
wearing the dunce's cap to deliver the things to the school.
I returned home after being criticized.*[168] *When I walked in
the door, Father said, "Let's have some* jiaozi *(dumplings)'."*

In the Tong home, jiaozi *were a treat. At a time when the
house had been ransacked and he'd been humiliated in the
ugliest manner possible, he'd deal with the dark mood that
settled over the house with the words, "Have some* jiaozi.*"*[169]

In 1968, Red Guards in the Architecture Department of
Nanjing Institute of Technology froze teachers' salaries, but were
told to restore them at year's end. When they lined up to receive
their pay, every "bourgeois professor and instructor" was slapped
by a Red Guard named Wang Caizhong. Tong was first in line.
Wang smacked the balding architect and barked: "Do you deserve
this much salary?" He said, "No," as he walked off with the money.

Before receiving their money, those whose salary had been
frozen were instructed to "earnestly declare their position"
regarding how they comprehended and carried out Party policy. In
October 1968, Tong Jun handed in his salary statement:

*As a highly paid member of the bourgeois intelligentsia,
as well as the college ruling class, I am complicit in
promoting the Khrushchev revisionist education line,
taking money while doing damage. The working class has
every right to be angry at me, and it is absolutely correct
and necessary for them to act and impose economic
sanctions. As I see it, freezing or releasing my salary now
was part of our re-education by the working class. This*

embodies the fundamental demand of Party policy, of reforming my worldview.[170]

Every time Tong Jun returned home after being struggled against, he picked up a book and started to read, as if nothing had happened. But there were paper seals on all the books and other printed material in the house, so he wrapped the cover of *Mao Zedong Selected Works*[171] around some of his books to keep them around.

Tong Jun's Cultural Revolution submissions

In Huang Yiluan's view:

Tong Jun was very politically conscious, his grasp as keen as any Communist Party member. He just shied away from talking about it. Given his taciturn attitude, he kept his opinions to himself, not drawing attention to himself, which enabled him to stay out of the rebels' sights. Neither a part of the revolutionary activities nor a target, he avoided getting involved; outside of actively carrying out his assigned work load, he spent the rest of his time reading and writing.[172]

Liu Guanghua, who had moved to the United States after the Cultural Revolution ended, recalled an incident from August 1967:

I had entertained the thought of ending my life. I was sweeping the area in front of the Architecture Department gate when Tong Jun came up and brushed past me, saying softly, "You mustn't think of killing yourself." That was hugely comforting to me, and my heart filled with tears of gratitude.[173]

Forty years later, Liu can still recall the look on Tong Jun's face and what he said. "In those days, no one felt safe, afraid of being hit while they were down. Not only was that single comment by Tong Jun a life vest, it instilled me with a fighting spirit. He saved my life."[174]

Liu Guanghua reveals Tong Jun's strategy regarding political movements in another of his recollections:

The college Party committee felt that vigor was lacking, so the department's Party secretary required every professor to write a big character poster with their view of educational reform. Tong Jun and I were office mates, so I asked this revered elder what to do. "Don't write anything," he said, terse and clear as always.

"Won't that keep me from getting past this?"
"There's nothing they can do to you if you write a self-
reflection, so write about your bourgeois views of
education." I had always considered Tong Jun to be my
mentor, and though he was not much of a talker, what little
he did say was persuasive. The next morning, I pasted up
a self-critical but perfunctory big-character poster, and
it did not result in my falling into the Party's trap. Yang
Tingbao conscientiously wrote out ten suggestions, and
was immediately criticized for "separating himself from
politics, preferring expert over red, placing technique in
command"—the sort of label that can apply in almost any
situation.[175]

According to Tong Wen, in 1969, Red Guards hauled Tong Jun up onto the platform at the entrance to the Nanjing Institute of Technology Architecture Department and made him kneel in front of the image of Chairman Mao as he held a copy of the treasured Red Book.[176] When the sixty-nine-year-old man got to his feet, he softly uttered the famous phrase *"Eppur si mouve"* (and yet it moves). The phrase was part of a "confession" read in Latin by Galileo[177] three hundred years ago in front of the Pope, on the steps of St. Peter's Basilica (Vatican City, Rome, Italy), on his knees, hands resting on the Bible; he had undergone twenty years of trial.

Tong Jun put up a reprint of Raphael's *Madonna del Granduca* behind the door by his bed. That act alone was enough to be labeled a counter-revolutionary. He had also asked his sons engaged in research on radios and semiconductors to put together a radio for him, so that in the still of the night he could listen to the Voice of America, the American radio network; listening to enemy broadcasts constituted a serious criminal act.

After the Cultural Revolution, Tong Jun said: "Fame and fortune mean next to nothing to me. Just being human is tiring enough, and those two words make it even worse, which is why I've had a few ups and downs in my life."[178]

Here is how Tong Wen analyzed his grandfather's actions during those extraordinary times:

*In an era when values were being destroyed, taking
refuge in seclusion was a relatively easy way to protect
his character and avoid the pitfalls and wreckage of the
world outside. Viewed from actual conditions of the time,
expecting every individual to stand up against evil during
absurd and cruel times is pure folly. Though people may
heap praise on Don Quixote[179] for his solitary fight against
evil, the harsh reality entails brutality and imprisonment
for an individual.[180]*

Tong Ming and Tong Wen had once even wondered if it was a sign of cowardice for Tong Jun to abandon his life in architecture and his hobby of nature sketches, and choose to live in seclusion during that transformative historical period. Or if it was more related to his having grown up in a transitional era, when "Expel the Tatars, Restore China"[181] was a call to action, with the Manchu becoming outcasts?

In his self-criticisms, Tong Jun often wrote that he was an individualist.

*My Individualism is not for fame or fortune, but is an even
more selfish individualism; it is both above and external
to fame and fortune—one that is "fiercely independent,"
it "stands aloof," "is standoffish," "and remains divorced
from convention," the standard assessment of character
held by intellectuals. Individualism based on fame and
fortune is a part of society still associated with the masses;
individualism not based on fame and fortune stands apart
from the masses. My anti-fame and fortune-renouncing
ideology is based on my appreciation of Yuan (dynasty)*

painting and late Ming literature. In Ni Zan's[182] scenic
paintings, for instance, you never see a person, just two or
three shriveled trees, some scattered boulders, and maybe
a pagoda, and I find that utterly intoxicating.[183]

In another self-criticism, he announced that he was cosmopolitan, but that in those days, "patriot" was the only choice.[184]

In Tong Jun's view, politics allowed only gains and losses, not right or wrong.

— CHAPTER TEN —

A Little Page Boy

Tong Wen was born in 1962. Tong Jun chose names for this grandson and for his granddaughter based on his wife's name before she was married.

From today's perspective, Tong Jun's marriage would be considered a standard arranged union. All the arrangements were made by his father, Enge.

Tong Linsu recalled:

In 1920, Grandfather brought my father and mother together in accordance with feudal traditions. She was a Manchu, an outstanding student at a girls' normal school. They did not have any affection for each other or get to know each until after they were married. Since Father was away at school, they were apart much of the time, but they grew closer as husband and wife. She helped him in his career, and even transcribed the manuscript for Jiangnan Yuanlin Zhi *in her own hand. Sadly, exhausted by a life of hard work, she died in 1956, which came as a real blow to Father. It occurred at a time when he was so seriously ill; he was unable to say good-bye, something he considered the greatest regret of his life. He kept a photo of her at the head of his bed, and never remarried.*[185]

Top: Center (standing): Tong Jun's wife Guan Weiran
Bottom: Tong Jun and his family, having recently arrived in
Shanghai in the early 1930s
(left to right) Guan Weiran, Tong Linsu, Tong Shibai, and
Tong Jun

Despite the reality that it was an arranged marriage, and that Tong Jun was a staunch male chauvinist as a young man, when he was studying and working in the United States and when he returned to China, he and his wife were a devoted couple. Their first son was born two years after they were married. When Tong Jun was in the United States, he sent his wife a photo, on the back of which he copied a poem by renowned poet Li Shangyin:

Lord, You ask when I'm coming home, I do not know.
On Sichuan Mountain, night rains swell autumn ponds.
When shall we again trim wicks by the western window and
talk together about rain falling on Sichuan Mountain?[186]

He later wrote a poem of his own:

I look in the mirror and see gray threads among the black,
My fondest dream is to stroll again in the garden.
Night rain falls beyond the western window, as my return is
delayed,
and I long to hear the heart-warming sounds of neighbors
laughing.[187]

Tong Wen also shared:

After Grandfather returned (from the United States),
Grandmother learned how to cook Western food. Our
tableware was mostly Western, and we had a foreign stove
and oven. In Nanjing, we even raised turkeys. Her Western
meals looked and tasted like the real thing, and I heard
words of praise from many friends of the family.[188]

Guan Weiran studied English with Tong Jun, and together, they watched Hollywood movies. According to Tong Shibai, "When Tong Jun went to Shanghai, Mother heard that it was a sort of sin city, and was concerned."[189] However, not long after, Tong Jun sent for his wife and children to join him.

When Tong Jun reminisced about his wife in his later years,[190] he considered himself a very lucky man to have had such a happy marriage. He cried bitterly for days and nights after she died in 1956, and did not get over the loss for years. Before Guan Weiran died, she asked Liu Dunzhen's wife to find a new wife for Tong Jun after she was gone. She raised only one condition—that it be a middle-aged, never-married-before lady. Chen Jing, Liu's wife, broached the topic with Tong Jun once, but only once, after seeing how his face fell that one time she brought it up. She could not have known that he had wrapped the urn holding his wife's ashes in her favorite, semi-transparent indigo qipao and kept it in the chest at the head of his bed until he died twenty-seven years later. Almost all her other dresses had been confiscated in house searches during the Cultural Revolution.

A widower at the age of fifty-five, Tong Jun had once famously said: "A man also ought to remain chaste."[191] Thirty years later, when he was being treated in Beijing, he told daughter-in-law number three, Gu Danyun (Tong Linbi's wife), to alter his wife's padded coats, trousers, and sleepwear to fit a man. He wore those altered winter clothes and sleepwear in the last years of his life.

His friends saw how living alone in Nanjing, he was unable to shed his grief over his wife's death, so Yang Tingbao used his connections to get Tong Linsu transferred to Nanjing to keep his father company. He was working with the Ministry of Defence at that time. Soon after Liberation, Linsu graduated from Peking University's Physics Department, where he did so well that he was sent to the Navy Section of the Ministry of Defence, assigned to Qian Sanqiang—known as the "father of China's atomic bomb"—as his assistant, undertaking research on the little-known neutron bomb, and later, writing a treatise on the decay of neutrons. On his return to Nanjing, he had to do research on topics unrelated to national defence, so he was assigned to the Department of Electronics at the Nanjing Institute of Technology, to undertake scientific research on electron display. Linsu's oldest, his son

Tong Jun and Guan Weiran during their time in the
northeast

Tong Wen, became his grandfather's most cherished companion, and earned the sobriquet "little page boy."

One day, Tong Wen's grade school-teacher had written his name as "Tong Shaowen," meaning lost Wen, so angering Tong Jun that he stormed over to the local police precinct to change his name back to Tong Wen. Interestingly, when naming their children, his third son, Tong Linbi chose "Tong Bing," meaning soldier, as his son's name. His younger brother Tong Yin chose the name "Tong Jun," meaning army, and "Tong Min," meaning people, for his sons. When Tong Jun learned what names they had chosen, he told them to change the characters in all three names to reflect less provocative meanings, especially given the troubled times.

Tong Wen recalls:

When I was born, Grandfather was over sixty, and by the time I had an idea about what life was all about, he was already very old. The person I stayed with all that time was a loving old man, a cultivator who did not allow himself to succumb to being tired.[192]

Tong Wen was a somewhat unruly child. A friend had once given Tong Jun an orchid plant, which he had treasured. By watering and tending it vigilantly, he had raised seven flowers, which put him in a good mood. Then, suddenly, one day they were all gone. The boy had plucked every one of the flowers and laid them out in a circle on the table, feeling quite proud of himself. Tong Jun was furious; he pulled a long face all day. But never once did he yell at, or strike any of the children in his family. On another occasion, Tong Wen kept pulling the cat's tail, giving the poor creature loose stools for days. Tong Jun was beside himself.

"You are born under the sign of the tiger," he said to Tong Wen. "A cat taught a tiger how to run and jump. As soon as the tiger learned how, it turned on the cat, to eat it. The cat ran up a tree. That was one trick it hadn't taught the tiger, so 'tigers' are not supposed to mistreat cats."[193]

Tong Jun doted on his cat. There are photos of him reading a newspaper with the cat curled up in his lap. Tong Wen elaborates on this family tale about cats and rats:

It seems, a cat and a rat had made a date to be named one of the twelve zodiac animals of the Chinese zodiac. On the road, the rat learned that eleven had already been decided, leaving space for only one more, so it quickened its pace and managed to grab the last spot. The cat would forever bear a grudge against the rat.[194]

Tong Jun was born in the year of the rat, and so he loved cats, a symbolic apology for an earlier slight. Tong Jun's cat was another of his cherished companions in his later years. He conversed with his cat often, and when he was in a particularly good mood, took pictures of it. They had once owned a dog; it appeared in a photograph with Tong Jun's wife, standing on its hind legs to rub its nose against her hand. But in 1952, the Neighborhood Committee came by and beat it to death.

When Tong Wen was taking the university entrance exam in 1980, his grandfather laid out a single proscription: "You may not go to Beijing."[195] When Tong Wen filled out his list for schools and departments, his first choice was the Radio Engineering Department at Nanjing Institute of Technology; the school's Architecture Department was second. He had discussed his preferences over and over with Tong Jun, who refused to offer an opinion. His posted exam scores were excellent, to the delight of the whole family, since that meant he'd get his first choice. His mother, Zhan Hongying, was a professor in the Radio Engineering Department. Tong Wen later came to learn that the day after the results were posted, Tong Jun donated his personal set square, T-square, and other drafting tools to the college's Architecture Department.

Yang Tingbao, Tong Wen, and Tong Jun

In reality, from early on in Tong Wen's childhood, Tong Jun gave the "little page boy" a systematic education, the bulk of it relating to a specialized background training in architecture. "He was always there with me," Tong Wen recalls, "from my bawling infancy to when I went to college."[196] One day Tong Wen said he wanted to read a book, and so his grandfather took him over to his bookcase and told him to pick any one that he wanted. He took out a book on architecture because it had a picture of a beautiful house on the cover. Tong Jun took a look: it was Frank Lloyd Wright's Fallingwater.[197] He was thrilled, and immediately explained to his grandson why it was such a fine house, making it sound like a beginner's class in architecture, but Tong Wen quickly lost interest.

160

Tong Wen's mother supervised her young son to practice writing Chinese characters under the grape trellis in the front yard. Though Tong Wen did it only to make her happy, Tong Jun was nonetheless delighted to watch the boy do as he was told. From then on, his favorite question was "Have you practiced your calligraphy?"

In middle school, two of his classmates wrote beautiful characters in two classical styles, which concerned Tong Wen, who asked Tong Jun for style sheets, which he found and showed to his grandson so he could choose the ones he wanted. Confused, the boy asked which was the best, so Tong Jun showed him samples of the famous Wang Xizhi's[198] calligraphy. After that, Tong Wen tried writing with a brush every day, sometimes joined by his grandfather, practicing the four most common styles from four most distinguished calligraphers in China.

Sharing his wisdom, Tong Jun said, "Calligraphy doesn't need a hundred days of practice, unlike painting." This led Tong Wen to assume that calligraphy was a snap, and that three months or so was all it took to master it, compared to painting, for which there was likely no time limit. Dubious, Tong Wen asked how he could write good-looking characters. Tong Jun looked at his practice sheet and said, "Don't focus on each individual stroke, since the precision is not important. The key is in the overall 'spirit' of the penmanship."

"This was one of the very few epiphanies I've experienced in my life," said a fifty-year-old Tong Wen.

I'm grateful to him for pinpointing the key issue, because I quickly became the top calligrapher, especially in fountain pen, in my class.[199]

At about that time, Tong Wen suddenly developed an interest in painting, but during those days, art paper was unavailable, so Tong Jun washed the watercolors off some of his and used them to give his grandson painting lessons. Yang Tingbao had visited Tong

Jun one of those days and was shocked by what he saw. In later years, anytime that his grandfather was mentioned, Tong Wen only sighed and said, "I was unworthy of his effort."[200]

Outside of his achievements in architectural theory and as an architect, Tong Jun's literary talent is generally overlooked. The truth is, from 1940 to 1944, he and his friends often wrote poetry to one another, and he printed *Xinan Yincao*.[201] Though he did not write much, for an architectural theorist, his poetic talents were surprisingly good. One such is his *Kuiwei Chun Ti Xiao Qingyun Xiong Hua (A Painting for Xiao Qingyun, in Spring)*, 1943:

> *The siege has not reached the book district;*
> *So I put myself among books;*
> *reciting back and forth amid the noise of ramming earthen*
> *walls;*
> *the homesick traveler fears the road back is blocked;*
> *an old farmer longing for rain is happy to see clouds;*
> *trying my hands on painting because of the greening*
> *mountains;*
> *being late turning on the lamp I rely upon the bright moon;*
> *when can I return home to be a fisherman;*
> *perch with a pot of liquor for a carefree life.*[202]

Tong Jun had his favorites in both poetry and painting. He told Tong Wen that he preferred the poet Du Fu over Li Bai, and the painter Huang Binhong over Qi Baishi. In a memorial for his good friend, Chen Zhi wrote, "He was extremely knowledgeable in music, especially symphonies."[203]

Here is how Tong Jun analyzed his hobby in his self-confession:

> *I was born into a bourgeois family and was nurtured*
> *on feudal thought as a child. As an adult, I received the*
> *enslavement education of American imperialists, and was*
> *particularly fond of capitalist culture, arts, and science*

*and technology, as well as Chinese classical literature
and art, immersing myself in it until it became elemental
nature. Treating it as a foundation to lead a settled life, I
developed a penchant for favoring the old and worshipping
the foreign.*[204]

The little page boy was truly lucky to have such a guide to life. After Tong Jun died, Tong Wen shared several vignettes from their life.

*It was a 1968 summer night, and I'd just turned six. My
uncle gave me an illustrated storybook called* Banye Ji
Jiao,[205] *about a landlord exploiting a young farm laborer.
It was a rarely encountered bilingual publication, with the
translation in English titled* The Cock Crows at Midnight.[206]
*When he saw what I was reading, Grandfather wore a
pained, pensive look. He asked me if I knew what the English
title meant. I shook my head. He said it was a famous saying
in the West. On the night before he was nailed to the cross,
at the Last Supper with his twelve disciples, Jesus made this
statement to his Jewish disciple Peter, who would deny him;
he said: "The cock crows at midnight. You must disavow me
in order to avoid being punished with me." Peter responded
tearfully that he would not denounce his faith.
The year 1968 was the peak of the Cultural Revolution
and the country was caught up in a "a sea of red."*[207]
*Humanity's most precious commodity, the conscience,
was tossed into the rubbish heap of history by an
entire nation. Grandfather was sweeping the floors and
watching the gate at his school, and all the books at home
had been sealed as banned reading. The story he told me
was one I've never forgotten, buried in my heart all these
many years, because back in those days, telling it would
have made us "counter revolutionaries."*

On that night in 1968, I began to understand what it took to live a proper life.

I started learning how to write when I entered middle school. I copied sentences like "the east wind blows;" "the red flag stands;" "the revolution is in excellent shape throughout the nation;" and so on, and was reprimanded by Grandfather.

"Writing is hard, it takes work," he said. "It must be a solid effort, filled with meaning and with clear authority. Stay away from meaningless phrases and empty words; avoid adjectives as much as possible, make it forceful, and revise over and over. Start by working on the organization of paragraphs, then of sentences, and end by polishing the words. Like composing a telegram."

He made me read something he'd just written. It was the introduction to Liu Dunzhen's Suzhou Gudian Yuanlin (Classical Gardens of Suzhou)*; just a mere few paragraphs. He told me it was his thirty-fourth draft. It was concise and easy to understand. It was a skillful work that traversed the history of Chinese gardens and theories about them. When Grandfather corrected drafts, he used an engraving tool and glue, so the manuscript pages were of uneven length. He was relentless in his revisions, sometimes even on page proofs. I recall part of the final version:*

"The late Ming work Yuan Ye *by Ji Cheng was taken to Japan in a handwritten copy with the title* Duo Tiangong. *Somewhat later, Zhu Shunshui*[208] *fled to Japan and took the Jiangnan garden-style with him."*

I did not know at the time that those few lines of his were built on years of hard work and his scholarship. He'd begun reading Yuan Ye[209] *in 1932, examining the various editions and the Japanese translation, because in his spare time while working at The Allied Architects, he studied*

*late Ming literature with a scholar of classical Chinese
literature. In Shanghai, he wrote fifty pages of notes on Zhu
Shunshui's work,*[210] *enough for two publishable scholarly
articles. And yet, he distilled it down to two sentences.
When his piece was finished, he signed it "Yang Tingbao."
When Yang read it, he told Grandfather it was perfect, with
but one suggestion: change the sentence "a contribution
to society" to "a contribution to socialism," in order to
more closely follow the times. Then he added Grandfather's
name—with Yang Tingbao as the primary author and Tong
Jun as the secondary author. The draft was finished.
This incident taught me what it meant to be a great scholar.
Grandfather taught me by personal example as much as
by instruction, letting circumstances dictate the course
of learning. I began studying classical Chinese after
graduating from high school, and was intrigued by it.
Grandfather started tutoring me, selecting outside texts
for me to read. He advocated focusing on the classics,
heightening my interest by adding some classical literary
essays. He insisted that I read and memorize three
essays from* Guwen Guanzhi: *"Ma Yuan Admonishes His
Brother's Sons, Ma Yan, and Ma Dun,"*[211] *"Preface to 'A
Banquet in Taoli Garden',"*[212] *and "Epitaph on a Lowly
Hut."*[213] *He and I settled on a study schedule of half an hour
every night before bedtime, between ten and ten-thirty. The
approach was unique: I read a section or two aloud, then
Grandfather explained the meaning. That is when I realized
the depth and breadth of his knowledge. He explained
difficult texts in simple terms and offered critiques that
really got me thinking. What impressed me was—in my
study of* Lunyu (The Analects)[214]—*how he described the
difference between people, the gentleman, and the petty
man. When studying* Laozi,[215] *Grandfather explained the*

relationships between the philosophical concepts dao
(the way) and qi *(tools),* ruanjian *(software), and* yingjian
(hardware); Einstein's fourth dimension, *and Hilbert's*
Infinite Space. *When studying* Zhuangzi,[216] *we discussed*
Jean-Paul Sartre's[217] existentialism, *and Immanuel*
Kant's[218] Pure Reason. *He took pains to tell me the story
of "Pao Ding dissecting an ox,"*[219] *a simple concept that
architects and engineers would do well to emulate. With*
Yijing[220] (The Book of Changes), *he talked about DNA and
human beings' natural talents.*
*Grandfather's hopes for me were that I be a good person
and a good scholar. To me, he was the epitome of what
it means to be both. In my immature mind, he was the
bright light of wisdom. When he left me forever, there
was an emptiness in my heart I thought I could never fill,
and confusion I thought would never be untangled. I talk
to him often, for to me, he still lives and never departs
this world.*[221]

In Tong Wen's narration of his experiences, has also jests
about frequent dreams he has of Tong Jun. "Grandpa shouts down
from upstairs: 'Where are you, Wen? Why aren't you studying?' I
hold a cricket jar close to me as I hide behind the sofa, afraid he'll
catch me."[222]

1925, Tong Jun on the eve of departing for the United States

— CHAPTER ELEVEN —

Jiangnan Yuanlin Zhi

In 1963, *Jiangnan Yuanlin Zhi* (*On Classical Gardens in Southeastern China*) was published.

In the five years from 1932 to 1937, Tong Jun spent every Sunday exploring one of the 109 private gardens in the twenty-seven counties and cities of Jiangsu and Zhejiang. He did it alone, and with no financial support. With transportation being so spotty, he relied primarily on his two feet to travel to what remained of the gardens in Jiangsu and Zhejiang. Some had fallen into ruin. He had to locate attendants to help him gain admittance. On two occasions, he was even reported to the local police as someone up to no good.

"Father was seldom home to rest on Sundays," Tong Shibai recalls.

His idea of rest was to take a camera to the Shanghai environs or along rail lines to explore gardens. Once in a while, he took me along. Some of the gardens were in ruins, abandoned by their owners. Father would explain to attendants why he was there, and give them a small tip, so that he could go in and take pictures. At first, he used a bulky Zeiss Ikon camera with the Kodak 116 film. Each negative was twice the size of twelve 120 negatives, so there was no need to enlarge them, and the images were very clear. Some of the images in Jiangnan Yuanlin Zhi were

Tong Jun, his wife Guan Weiran, and son Tong Shibai, in a garden

taken with this camera. After a while, he felt that it was getting in the way, plus the developing costs were too high, so he bought a Leica for more than two hundred yuan, which used 135 film. Mother told me that two hundred yuan was a major outlay at the time—the cost of fifty bags of flour, at least. But she supported father's decision on the purchase. Because of that, many images of old gardens were recorded for posterity.[223]

In the summer of 1937, Tong Jun completed the manuscript for *Jiangnan Yuanlin Zhi*. Liu Dunzhen personally took it to Beijing to be printed by the SRCA. Liu and Liang Sicheng assumed that the society had by then wrapped up research on the imperial buildings in North China. Liu had come to the south to open up a new area of study, and Tong Jun was his Shanghai host. This was their first meeting. They had been corresponding for quite a while regarding bucket arches and textual research. Tong Jun told Liu that he had explored and mapped nearly a hundred Jiangnan gardens, and had completed a manuscript entitled *Jiangnan Yuanlin Zhi*, and that he was looking for a tour guide publisher. Liu recommended the SRCA.

According to Liu Zhiping[224] (Tong Jun's student from the first batch of architecture students who graduated from Northeastern University), *Jiangnan Yuanlin Zhi* was passed around among Liang Sicheng, Liu Dunzhen, and Zhu Qiqian[225] (founder of the SRCA), who were all astounded by what they read. It forged a new path and, thanks to a single man's efforts, created a complete theoretical framework, leaving little to do for those who come after. They discussed whether to publish the work in the society's (SRCA's) journal[226] as a special issue, or as a separate volume, in the nature of the *Qing Shi Yingzao Zeli*.[227] As an original work of scholarship, *Jiangnan Yuanlin Zhi* did not fit the society's traditional research paradigm, which was to focus on textual research and footnotes for *Yingzao Fashi* by Li Jie.[228] In the end, Zhu Qiqian decided to publish it as a book and asked Liang Sicheng to invite Tong Jun to join the society.

Liu Zhiping was one of Tong Jun's students who fled the Japanese from Northeastern University, whom he had personally taught in his own house. He became Liang Sicheng and Liu Dunzhen's assistant in the Society for Research in Chinese.

On May 17, 1937, Liang Sicheng finished reading *Jiangnan Yuanlin Zhi*, in Beijing and wrote a long letter to Tong Jun, giving him high praise for an excellent manuscript:

> *I'm beyond impressed, now that I've read it. One: you were able to find time to complete the work despite your busy schedule in Shanghai. Two: the work is very thorough and includes many one-dimensional surveyors' maps. Three: you have searched out so much literature on the subject. Four: the writing is concise and clear, in the style of a Ming writer. Five: The writing itself makes clear*

how devoted the author is toward gardens; not a mere observer, but someone who deeply appreciates the art of gardens. Without any doubt, it is a meticulously conceived masterpiece. There are, I believe, two flaws that mar the perfection. One: in the manuscript you rarely refer to the photographs or drawings. There are a number of revealing photographs, but you failed to refer to them; the separation of text and illustration is regrettable. I believe that Liu Dunzhen mentioned this in his letter. Two: in the "Present Condition" section, considerable importance has been placed on the garden histories, but personal impressions are in short supply. You have largely avoided including how you felt about the structures and the general layout in the gardens you visited. I'd like to know your reactions to these two concerns. After Zhu (Qiqian) finished reading this major work, not only was he full of praise, but he is also entertaining ideas of inviting you to join the society to engage in archaeological work.[229]

Liang Sicheng assumed that after leaving Northeastern University, Tong Jun wrote in his newly acquired late Ming Tongcheng School style.

After writing his letter, Liang Sicheng, along with Lin Huiyin (his wife) and their assistant, Mo Zongjiang, set off on another visit to Wutai Mountain in Shanxi Province, where they discovered the Foguang Temple, a wooden structure from the Tang dynasty. This amazing discovery was more than just the crowning glory of the SRCA; it was the pinnacle of Liang and Lin's scholarly careers.

The Marco Polo Bridge Incident[230] occurred while *Jiangnan Yuanlin Zhi* was being prepared for publication, so Zhu Qiqian took Tong Jun's manuscript, photographs, and surveyor maps to Tianjin, where he placed them in a safety deposit box in the British Standard Chartered Bank. Against all odds, the entire lot was destroyed when Tianjin was flooded the next year. This epoch-making work by (then) thirty-seven-year-old Tong Jun was just a few months short of being published, in the year 1937. However, due to the turn of events, it would not be until a quarter of a century later, in 1963, during the author's sixty-third year, that the work finally appeared in print—seven years after his wife, who had hand-written his manuscripts, had died.

During his sixth decade, Tong Jun once again sketched the gardens he had visited before the war with Japan. Though it was years later, in his mind's eye he could still see every stone and every tree in all the Jiangnan gardens he had visited, so that not only were his maps accurate, but were now invested with increased understanding. "As to the gardens, of which more than ten are well known, I am familiar with every pebble in each one of them."[231] An article published later compared his walking surveys of the gardens with later versions taken with surveyor tools, and found his to be more compelling.

Once *Jiangnan Yuanlin Zhi* was published, copies were sent to Beijing.

On December 15, 1963, after Zhu Qiqian received a copy, he was so excited that he immediately wrote to Tong Jun:

> *Separated north to south, I send my thoughts to you.*
> *Every time that Liu Shineng [Liu Dunzhen] and Yang*
> *Tingbao came to Beijing, they asked about the publication*
> *of* Jiangnan Yuanlin Zhi, *which was undertaken thirty*
> *years ago by the SRCA. The devastating Marco Polo*
> *Bridge Incident stopped the process. The Beijing branch*
> *of Commercial Press abandoned all responsibility by*
> *returning the manuscript without printing it; an unexpected*
> *setback. After the society moved south, your manuscript*
> *was destroyed in a flood; I did not fulfill my promise to you*
> *and felt terrible about letting you down. After examining*

the surviving pages of the original, I sent them to Liu
Shineng in Nanxi [Sichuan Province] to find a way to keep
them safe and, when convenient, return them to the author.
Later, Shineng took them with him to Nanjing and wrote
to tell me he'd returned the original manuscript to you,
but that some of the photographs were waterlogged and
blurred. The author would have to sort through, organize,
and add explanations. A ninety-year-old decrepit like me
had a chance to read a new book, whose quality doubled
that of the manuscript from thirty years before, with
improved printing that makes for better reading for these
old eyes. A great work, once delayed, has so excited me I
hesitate to lay it down.[232]

When Liang Sicheng laid eyes on his schoolmate's work, after
a quarter of a century, he wrote:

Yesterday, I received a copy of Jiangnan Yuanlin Zhi *from*
[Tong] Shibai, to my great delight. As you pointed out, the
true value of the book lies in your hand-drawn sketches
of the gardens, many of which no longer exist or have
undergone changes. The photographs, too, are hard-to-
come-by archival material.
Back when your manuscript was about to be published,
the Marco Polo Bridge Incident and the later flood
brought that to an end. Seeing the finished book now
gives me great pleasure. When I gave it a quick read back
then, a lack of experience cramped my understanding.
After Liberation, I made two or three trips to Suzhou,
Wuxi, and Yangzhou; they were just brief stays that
made it all right to say I'd been there, but gave me a
general perception of the sites. Now, with a little more
understanding, after rereading it, I am impressed with
what you've done. But as someone with little knowledge of

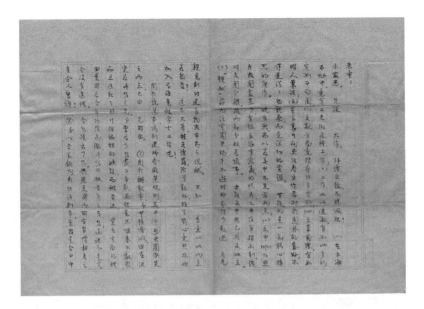

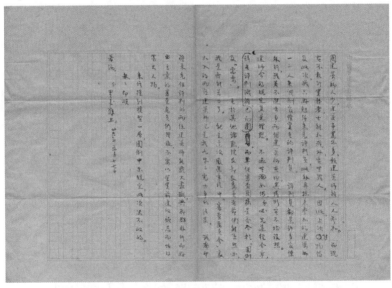

Liang Sicheng's letters to Tong Jun regarding *Jiangnan Yuanlin Zhi*

gardens, I look forward to a more incisive reading to fully appreciate its profound qualities.[233]

In his preface to *Jiangnan Yuanlin Zhi*, Liu Dunzhen wrote:

When the Chinese Architecture Research Group was formed in 1953, we suffered a serious lack of archival materials; old gardens were under reconstruction all over the country, and the ravages of war meant scant extant specimens. I urged the author of the current volume to glean what was left from water and insect damage and prepare for reprinting. The entire process was truly filled with twists and turns. There is more I would like to say here, as I personally took part in its completion over two decades.[234]

His words attest to the difficulty of publishing the volume. Zhao Chen and Tong Wen once wrote an article analyzing how *Jiangnan Yuanlin Zhi* managed to come out in the 1960s:

After the Architectural Engineering Bureau held a "Forum on Residential Construction Standards and the Art of Architecture" in May 1959, ideas in architecture began to once again thrive throughout the country. An editorial titled "Let All Schools Speak out and Architectural Creativity Flourish"[235] appeared in the March 1962 issue of Architecture Journal. *In the same month, Vice Premier Chen Yi spoke at the national conference on scientific work, at which he conducted a "hat removal ceremony" for intellectuals, that is, removing the label of bourgeois intellectual, and affirming them as "people's intellectuals" and "mental workers for the proletariat." All this aided a revival in publishing. Liu Dunzhen crafted an elaborate introduction[236] for the book, not only striving to demonstrate the old work's significance in the new society, but also*

attempting to elevate its author's "political awareness."
Hence it was finally and formally published in 1963. [237]

In his own introduction from the 1930s, Tong Jun wrote:

Rather than increasing in numbers, traditional gardens in
our country were dwindling. Every time I found myself in a
famous one, I could not help but linger with great emotion,
forgetting to eat all day. I was besieged by sorrow over all
the lovely scenery lying in waste like an aging beauty. As
they are declining, we must treasure every blade of grass
and every (tree) limb, so they will not be swept away by the
torrent of time. [238]

His devotion to these gardens shone through the text.

When finishing the manuscript in the spring of 1937, Tong
Jun added archival literature from historical figures such as Ban
Gu, Liu Yiqing, Wang Shizhen, Li Yu, Shen Fu, and many more.
Tong Jun's intellectual capacity went beyond our imagination when
we consider how, in the political climate of the time, he managed
to establish an area of studies in his spare time.

When writing the first chapter of *Jingnan Yuanlin Zhi*, it
seems like Tong Jun was conducting a spiritual correspondence
with his teacher, Wang Guowei. In his overview of the book,
Tong offered the idea of three realms: the first realm—proper
density; the second realm—adequate curves; and the third—
a view ahead. He did not offer excessive explications on these
realms, and actually used the phrase "a garden likely with three
realms," [239] in reference to some of the gardens, which does not
come across as confident.

In his *Renjian Cihua*, [240] Wang Guowei used "three realms of
life" to describe how "those who carry out impressive deeds or
acquire great learning—past and present—all experience three
states: one—'Last night, the western wind denuded the jade tree,

I went up to the tower alone and looked into the distance;' two—'My belt was getting loose, but I have no regret, as I turned wan and sallow for her;' and three—'I searched for her in the crowd, when I chanced to turn back to look, she was standing where the light was dim.'

With its outstanding prose and profound and lofty concepts, *Jiangnan Yuanlin Zhi* became an unsurpassable classic for scholars of traditional gardens. The writer Huang Shang wrote:

> In this one book, one not only sees why the author's views and arguments make it a ground-breaking classic of scholarship on traditional Chinese gardens, but can also appreciate his beautiful prose, reminiscent of reading Luoyang Temples before the Raid.[241] No later work has come close by comparison.
>
> "Qing qu"—affection and interest—are two words uttered by Prof. Tong, which sound ethereal, but have a staying quality, for they brighten up colors and create redolence that never end in life.[242]

The concepts of purpose and interest were the most important things Wang Shu learned as an architect, something he got from Tong Jun's first book on gardens, *Dongnan Yuanshu*.

> After rereading it six times in 1997, I found it so delightful, I took out his Jiangnan Yuanlin Zhi *for another reading, and that was when the two words leapt into my field of vision and went straight to my heart.*[243]

Tong Jun's great-granddaughter, Yang Yongsheng, got curious about gardens just before going to college, so she opened her great-grandfather's book and underlined noteworthy passages based on her reading training. To her surprise, she found nearly every sentence was worthwhile and hardly a single word could be overlooked. In fact, she discovered the most prominent feature of her great grandfather's writing style:

Judicious and rigorous selection of materials, copious
quotations and extensive citations, and precise and concise
analysis, with no superfluous expressions, to the point that
the prose cannot be pared down any further.[244]

I wonder how Tong Jun, wherever he is, would react to her comments.

After a failed attempt at publishing *Jiangnan Yuanlin Zhi* in the 1930s, Tong Jun put it on the backburner. When Liu Dunzhen's Chinese Ancient Architecture Research Group planned to publish the result of their study, *Classical Gardens of Suzhou*,[245] the publisher approached Tong Jun, but he "had no plans to renew the viewpoints in his own old work, not even revise the classical Chinese he used."[246]

As for all the admiration, praise, and surprise lavished on him, we have reason to believe that Tong Jun would be expressionless, regardless, just as he was most of the time. The publication of *Jiangnan Yuanlin Zhi* was delayed for several decades, but he never showed a sign of giving up; likewise, he did not appear particularly pleased when his work finally came out.

Liu Dunzhen died in 1968 long before the second printing of *Jiangnan Yuanlin Zhi* was being planned in 1981. To memorialize his decades-long friend and colleague, Tong Jun asked Liu's son, Liu Xujie, to write a preface for the second edition. As Tong Jun— the foremost researcher in Chinese gardens—was well versed in both Chinese and Western scholarship, young Liu Xujie was apprehensive about writing a preface for such an important work. Tong Jun had only two demands: use classical Chinese, and use traditional characters for the new edition. Liu was overjoyed after turning in the essay, for Tong Jun changed only two words before it went to press. Hence the first edition of *Jiangnan Yuanlin Zhi* in 1963 had an introduction from Liu Dunzhen and a second one in 1982, by Liu and Liu's son.

Based on Liu Xujie's recollection[247] of the time of the Cultural Revolution, Yang Tingbao, Liu Dunzhen, and Tong Jun had all suffered grievously during struggle sessions, with various accusations—one of which was studying gardens of the landlord class. Tong Jun was paraded on campus and out on the streets, during which time his accusers hit his exposed head with clubs. The three gentlemen were slandered as "three stinking plaques." Liu Dunzhen did not make it through and died in 1968.

In Tong Jun's self-criticism penned in November 1968, he wrote:

> *We were in the same boat, so we helped each other, we wallowed in the mire together, and we shared vile habits ... Liu and I had similar inclinations, so in 1964 he asked me to spend a week with him in Suzhou to help with his design. In addition, he often borrowed materials I had bought in the 1930s, and I was more than eager to share. I helped him start an unhealthy trend, with the belief that it was everyone's duty to promote cultural heritage ... I never criticized him for wasting national construction funds on his own personal hobbies, nor did I point out the residual, detrimental quality in these playthings of the feudal scholar-officials and members of the bourgeoisie. We liked the same things, so I couldn't be harsh on him while gentle on myself.*[248]

"In his later years, when he called to ask about my father's premature death," shared Liu Xuijie, "at one point, Mr. Tong sighed deeply and said, 'He was too thin-skinned.'"[249]

Tong Jun insisted on using traditional characters and a top-to-bottom printing style when *Jiangnan Yuanlin Zhi* was being published in 1960s—for which he had to write self-criticisms repeatedly during the Cultural Revolution. Fifty years later, when a reprint was underway, his grandson Tong Ming, who is an architecture scholar, once again rejected the publisher's suggestion to use simplified characters and actually asked to use the original font and typesetting. The book went through considerable complications and setbacks in the writing and publication process, a seemingly karmic mirroring of its author's life and experience.

In Tong Wen's view:

Suzhou gardens, or all gardens south of the Yangtze River, represented a dream world to Tong Jun, and his last visit to these gardens took place before the fall of Shanghai. After that, he couldn't find the courage to return, even when he was just a stone's throw away. But whenever he had an opportunity, he asked about their current conditions, worried that they might have been destroyed during Japanese bombings, the civil war, land reforms, and

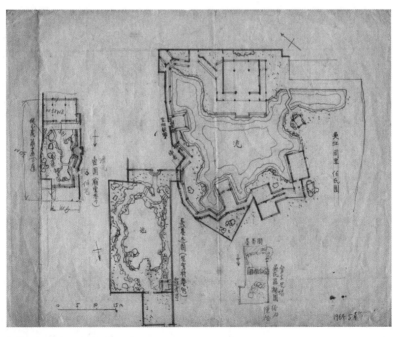

A sketch of a garden by Tong Jun

183

the calamitous Cultural Revolution. He seemed to place more importance on their continued existence than on his own survival. If the gardens remained, but their beauty and charm marred, that in itself would be a disaster, in his view. One hope in his life was to retain their distant, dreamy realms.[250]

Tong Jun reminds us of a phrase from the Bible:

"I have fought the good fight, I have finished the race, I have kept the faith. Now the crown of righteousness is upon me." (2 Timothy 4:7–8)

— AFTERWORD —

Tong Wen once asked me why I wanted to write about his grandfather and to what purpose. I could not answer him back then, nor can I now.

Was I writing a book? To me, it was a mere archival work, piecing together the recollections of interconnected people within the confines of my research.

Tong Jun left behind a large quantity of writing and materials. I thought he wouldn't care if I, or anyone else, wrote something about him, which was why I was able to stay in a relaxed mode. I don't care if no one wants to read this book or who its readers might be, nor do I care about the readers' reactions; good or bad, it doesn't concern me. But I was still on edge when Qin Lei[251] told me that she planned to include my work in a publication project and that it could be important to study topics on the architect Tong Jun.

As a matter of fact, I don't understand Tong Jun at all. I first met him one summer evening in 1990, when I passed down a long, narrow hallway and pushed open the living room door; I was startled to see him glaring at me from a wall mirror frame.

Few outside the field knew who he was, but even among those in the field who knew him, few understood him.

From the vantage point of time, some people and some matters gradually gain clarity, while others slowly blur. All I've done is keep a record, some of which is verifiable, while some might be self-contradictory; not to mention, the process was a mixture of joy and suffering. Documenting Tong Jun may serve to rouse us out of the fog of history.

I have too many to thank for this book, and I must beg their forgiveness for not listing them all here.

—Zhang Qin

— NOTES —

1. Wang Guowei 王国维, "Shashibi Zhuan" 莎士比传 [Biography of Shakespeare], in *Wang Guowei Wenji* 王国维文集 *[Collection of Wang Guowei"s Writings]*, eds. Yao Ganming 姚淦铭 and Wang Yan 王燕 (Beijing, China: Zhongguo Wenshi Chubanshe 中国文史出版社 China Culture and History Press, 1997) 3:394. See also note 51.

2. Xiang Bingren 项秉仁 profile page, DDB Shanghai website, accessed September 19, 2022, http://www.ddb.net.cn/list/12.

3. Tong Jun 童寯, *Tong Jun Wenji* 童寯文集 *[Collection of Tong Jun's Writings]* (Beijing, China: Zhongguo Jianzhu Gongye Chubanshe 中国建筑工业出版社 China Architecture & Building Press, 2006) 4:429.

4. Liang Sicheng 梁思成 (1901–1972) was a Chinese architect and architectural historian. He founded the Architecture Department of Northeastern University 东北大学, Shenyang, China and Tsinghua University 清华大学, Beijing, China, and was even awarded an honorary doctoral degree by Princeton University, United States; Else Glahn, "Liang Sicheng," Grove Art Online, 2003, https://www.oxfordartonline.com/groveart/search?siteToSearch=groveart&q=Liang+Sicheng&searchBtn=Search&isQuickSearch=true.

5. William Shakespeare, *Macbeth*, 5.5.2,374–2,379, Open Source Shakespeare, accessed September 18, 2022, https://www.opensourceshakespeare.org/.

6. *Zhongguo Da Baike Quanshu: Jianzhu, Yuanlin, Chengshi Guihua* 中国大百科全书: 建筑, 园林, 城市规划 *[The Encyclopedia of China: Architecture, Garden, Urban Planning]* (Beijing, China: Zhongguo Da Baike Quanshu Chubanshe 中国大百科全书出版社 Encyclopedia of China Publishing House, 1988), s.v. "Jiangnan Yuanlin" 江南园林 *[Gardens in Southeastern China]*.

7. Qi Kang 齐康, "Yi Tong Lao" 忆童老 [Recollections of Tong Jun], in *Guanyu Tong Jun* 关于童寯 *[About Tong Jun]*, eds. Tong Ming 童明 and Yang Yongsheng 杨永生 (Beijing, China: Zhishi Chanquan Chubanshe 知识产权出版社 Intellectual Property Publishing House and Zhongguo Shuili Shuidian Chubanshe 中国水利水电出版社 China Hydro Press, 2002), 26. See "Professor Qi Kang, Academician of Chinese Academy of Sciences," Southeast University, accessed September 18, 2022, https://www.seu.edu.cn/english/2019/0109/c22451a257830/page.htm.

8. Yan Longyu 晏隆余, "Gaofeng Liangjie, Bogu Tongjin: Daonian Tong Jun Xiansheng" 高风亮节, 博古通今——悼念童寯先生 [Exemplary Conduct and Nobility of Character, Timelessness of Knowledge and Wisdom—In Memory of Tong Jun], in *Guanyu Tong Jun*, 52.

9. Xiang Bingren, interview with the author, 2017.

10. Tanaka Tan 田中淡, *Chūgoku Kenchiku No Rekishi* 中国建筑 的历史 *[History of Chinese Architecture]* (Tokyo, Japan: Heibonsha 平凡社, 1981); Tanaka Tan, *Chūgoku No Ko Kenchiku* 中国的古建筑 *[Ancient Architecture in China]* (Tokyo, Japan: Kōdansha 讲谈社, 1980).

11. Guwen Guanzhi 古文观止 is a collection of high-standing literary works from the Spring and Autumn Period (770–476, BCE) to the late Ming dynasty (1368–1644) and was first printed in 1695; Wu Chucai 吴楚材 and Wu Tiaohou 吴调侯, eds., *Guwen Guanzhi [Gems of Chinese Classical Prose]* (Beijing, China: Zhonghua Shuju 中华书局 Zhonghua Book Company, 1959).

12. Tong Wen 童文, personal correspondence with the author, 2016.

13. Guo Husheng 郭湖生 (1931–2008) was an architectural historian and professor at Southeast University, Nanjing, China. See Cao Xun, "Shangdao Guo Husheng Xiansheng" 伤悼郭湖生先生 [Grieve for Guo Husheng], Jianzhushi 建筑师 *[The Architect]*, no. 157 (2008):104–107.

14. Tong Wen, personal correspondence with the author, 2015.

15. Xiang Bingren, personal correspondence with the author, 2017.

16. Xiang Bingren is referring to himself (in comparison to Tong Jun), but he also seemed to have in mind other teachers he had been taught by.

17. Zhong Xunzheng 钟训正 (born 1929) is an architect and professor at Southeast University, Nanjing, China; Zhong Xunzheng profile page, Architectural Design and Its Theory, Southeast University, accessed September 18, 2022, https://arch.seu.edu.cn/2018/0807/c16758a235166/page.htm.

18. Fang Yong 方拥, "Yinyi De Zhizhe: Jianzhu Dashi Tong Jun De Zuihou Sanshi Nian" 隐逸的智者: 建筑大师童寯的最后三十年 [The Wise Recluse—The Last Thirty Years of Architect Tong Jun], lecture at Banceng Bookstore 半层书店, Shanghai, China, August 19, 2017.

19. Wang Tingfang 王廷芳 was an ear, nose, and throat specialist; see: https://www.haodf.com/hospital/489/keshi/44199/jieshao.html and http://60.205.204.74/result/medicine/person/utvcubusvzqz/all/ (accessed September 18, 2022).

20. Lin Tianhong 林天宏, "Tong Jun: Bujin Renqing de Jianzhushi" 童寯: 不近人情的建筑师 [Tong Jun: An Uncompromising Architect], in Zhongguo Qingnian Bao 中国青年报 *China Youth Daily*, July 26, 2006.

21. Tong Wei 童蔚 , *Zhi Yiwei Jianzhushi* 致一位建筑师 *[To An Architect]*, personal correspondence with the author, 2017. Translated into English for the present publication by Carolyn Yao and Sofia Tong.

22. The Cultural Revolution was a sociopolitical movement led by Mao Zedong, the head of the Chinese Communist Party, that denounced the traditional and capitalistic ways of Chinese life, and lasted from 1966 to 1976. See also note 58 explaining "confessions" and "confessional material," also known as "self-criticisms." See also note 159.

23. Tong Jun, "Wenge Cailiao" 文革材料 [Documents During the Cultural Revolution] in *Tong Jun Wenji*, 4:380.

24. Yan Longyu 晏隆余 , "Gaofeng Liangjie, Bogu Tongjin: Daonian Tong Jun Xiansheng" in *Guanyu Tongjun*, 52.

25. Fang Yong 方拥 , "Yinyi de Zhizhe: Jianzhu Dashi Tong Jun de Zuihou Sanshi Nian."

26. H. G. Wells, *The Outline of History: Being a Plain History of Life and Mankind* (1920; California, United States: CreateSpace Independent Publishing Platform, 2018), printed in Chinese as H. G. Weiersi 韦尔斯 , *Shijie Shi Gang* 世界史纲 , trans. Liang Sicheng, 1927 (Shanghai, China: Shanghai Renmin Chubanshe 上海人民出版社 Shanghai People's Publishing House, 2006).

27. Fang Yong, "Gen Tong Jun Xiansheng Dushu." 跟童寯先生读书 [Follow Tong Jun] in *Guanyu Tong Jun*, 82.

28. Zhu Xi 朱熹 (1130-1200), "Yiluo Yuanyuanlu" 伊洛渊源录 [The Origins of the Yi-Luo School] in *Zhu Xi Quanshu* 朱熹全书 *[The Complete Works of Zhu Xi]*, eds. Zhu Jieren, Yan Zuozhi, and Liu Yongxiang(Shanghai, China: Shanghai Guji Chubanshe 上海古籍出版社 Shanghai Classics Publishing House and Anhui Jiaoyu Chubanshe 安徽教育出版社 Anhui Educational Publishing House, 2010), 12.

29. Zhu Guangting 朱光庭 (1037–1094) was a Yuanyou coalition member in the Song dynasty; Zhu Guangting profile page, Geni, accessed November 30, 2022, https://www.geni.com/people/Zhu-Guangting- 朱光庭 /6000000074746813103.

30. Yan Longyu 晏隆余 , "Gaofeng Liangjie, Bogu Tongjin: Daonian Tong Jun Xiansheng." in *Guanyu Tong Jun*, 56.

31. Tong Wen, personal correspondence with the author, 2015.

32. Tong Jun 童寯 , *Zaoyuan Shi Gang* 造园史纲 *[The Outline of Garden History]* (Beijing, China: Zhongguo Jianzhu Gongye Chubanshe, 1983).

33. Huang Yiluan 黄一鸾 , "Tong Xiansheng de Renge Meili" 童先生的人格魅力 Professor Tong's Charisma, in *Guanyu Tong Jun*, 101.

34. Tong Jun 童寯 , *Dongnan Yuanshu* 东南园墅 *[Glimpses of Gardens in Eastern China]* (Beijing, China: Zhongguo Jianzhu Gongye Chubanshe, 1997).

35. Tong Wen, personal correspondence with the author, 2015.

36. Tong Jun 童寯 , *Jiangnan Yuanlin Zhi* 江南园林志 *[On Classical Gardens in Southeastern China]* (Beijing, China: Zhongguo Jianzhu Gongye Chubanshe, 1963).

37. Zhu Guangya 朱光亚 (born 1942) is an architect and professor at Southeast University; http://www.jssks.com/index.php?c=article&id=5251.

38. Zhu Guangya 朱光亚 , "Xunzhang Zhaiju Shi Tong Jun" 寻章摘句 识童寯 [Know Tong Jun Through His Writing Paragraphs and Sentences] in *Guanyu Tong Jun*, 80.

39. Tong Wen, personal correspondence with the author, 2017.

40. Wang Shu 王澍 (born 1964) is a professor at the China Academy of Art 中国美院 , Hangzhou, China, and the winner of the 2012 Pritzker Architecture Prize in 2012; Louisiana Museum of Morden Art, ed., *Wang Shu Amateur Architecture Studio* (Zurich, Switzerland: Lars Müller Publishers, 2017).

41. Tong Jun 童寯 , *Tong Jun Wenxuan* 童寯文选 *[Selected Works of Chuin Tung]* (Nanjing, China: Dongnan Daxue Chubanshe 东南大学出版社 Southeast University Press, 1993).

42. Wang Shu 王澍 , "Zhiyou Qingqu" 只有情趣 [Just for Pleasure] in *Dongnan Yuanshu* 东南园墅 *[Glimpses of Gardens in Eastern China]* (Changsha, China: Hunan Meishu Chubanshe 湖南美术出版社 Hunan Fine Arts Publishing House, 2018), 5–14.

43. Wang Shu, 2012 Pritzker Architecture Prize Laureate acceptance note, The Pritzker Architecture, accessed September 28, 2022, https://www.pritzkerprize.com/cn/node/957.

44. Yang Yongsheng (1931–2012) was a publisher on architecture and former chief editor of *Jianzhushi* 建筑师 *[The Architect]*, as well as former deputy editor of *Zhongguo Jianzhu Gongye Chubanshe*. See Zhou Yi 周谊 "Huainian Yiwei Chuse De Bianjijia" 怀念一位出色的建筑编辑家 [In Memory of an Excellent Architecture Editor] in *Keji Yu Chuban* 科技与出版 *[Science-Technology & Publication]* (Beijing, China: Qinghua Daxue Chubanshe Youxian Gongsi 清华大学出版社有限公司 Tsinghua University Press, 2012) 10:73–74.

45. Liu Dunzhen 刘敦桢 (1897–1968) was an architectural historian and educationalist and colleague of Tong Jun at Central University, renamed the Nanjing Institute of Technology.

46. Liu Dunzhen, *Suzhou Gudian Yuanlin* 苏州古典园林 *[Classical Gardens of Suzhou]* (Beijing, China: Zhongguo Jianzhu Gongye Chubanshe, 1979), whose English edition was later published by SDX Joint Publishing in Hong Kong.

47. Tong Jun, "Suzhou Gardens" in *Tong Jun Wenxuan*, 117.

48. Tong Wen, personal correspondence with the author, 2015.

49. Tong Jun 童寯 , "Jianzhu Jiaoyu" 建筑教育 [The Architectural Education] in *Tong Jun Wenji*, 1:113.

50. Liang Qichao 梁启超 (1873–1929) was the father of Liang Sicheng and a prominent politician and educationalist. See Bai Limin, "Liang Qichao," Oxford Bibliographies, last modified August 30, 2016, doi: 10.1093/OBO/9780199920082-0136.

51. "Wang Guowei," Biography, Britanica online, accessed September 25, 2022, https://www.britannica.com/biography/Wang-Guowei.

52. Zhao Yuanren (1892–1982) was a Chinese modern linguist and musicologist. See Randy Lapolla, "Chao, Y. R. [Zhào Yuánrèn] 赵元任 (1892–1982)," Encyclopedia of Chinese Language and Linguistics, accessed September 26, 2022, http://dx.doiorg/10.1163/2210-7363_ecll_COM_000028.

53. Chen Yinque (1890–1969) was a Chinese educationalist and scholar. See Zhang Longxi, "Literary Modernity in Perspective," in *A Companion to Modern Chinese Literature*, ed. Zhang Yingjin (New Jersey, United States: John Wiley & Sons, 2015), accessed September 26, 2022, https://ebookcentral.proquest.com/lib/cuhk-ebooks/reader.action?docID=2075675&ppg=59.

54. Hu Shi (1891–1962) was a thinker, litterateur, philosopher, and the most influential and controversial scholar in modern China. See Bai Jian 白吉庵 , *Hu Shi: Zhenshi De Weiwo* 胡适: 真实的为我 *[The True Self]* (Taipei, Taiwan: Wu Nan Tushu Chuban Gufen Youxian Gongsi 五南图书出版股份公司 Wu-Nan Book Inc., 2013) .

55. Wang Guowei, "Renjian Cihua" 人间词话 ["Poetic Remarks on the Human World"], in *Wang Guowei Wenji*, 1:147.

56. Chen Yinque 陈寅恪 , "Qinghua Daxue Wang Guantang Xiansheng Jinian Beiming" 清华大学王观堂先生纪念碑铭 [Inscription on the Monument to Mr. Wang Guantang at Tsinghua University], in *Jin Ming Guan Conggao Erbian* 金明馆丛稿二编 *[The Second Edited Drafts Clusters at Jinming Hall]* (Shanghai, China: Shanghai Guji Chubanshe, 1980), 218.

57. Tong Wen, personal correspondence with the author, 2015.

58. Disclosure documents or *jiaodai cailiao* are also known as "confessions" and refer to forced written confessions or self-criticisms from the subject enforced by the government. See Tong Jun, *Tong Jun Wenji*, 4: 374–380.

59. Tong Jun, "Zhi Wilma Xin" 致 Wilma 信 [Letters to Wilma], in *Tong Jun Wenji*, 4:430.

60. This department subsequently became a part of the Nanjing Institute of Technology.

61. Wu Liangyong (born 1922) was a student of Tong Jun; Wu Liangyong, personal correspondence with the author, 2016.

62. Lin Zhu, interview with the author, 2016.

63. Tong Wei, personal correspondence with the author, 2017.

64. A struggle session was a popular practice during the Cultural Revolution that was a violent public spectacle—usually conducted on a stage, in an auditorium, or at the workplace—where "class enemies" against the Maoists were publicly tortured and humiliated, sometimes ending in the death of the victim. The victims were usually tortured or beaten by people they were close to: friends and spouses pressured into betraying one another, students pitted against teachers, and even children manipulated into exposing their parents.

65. A letter from Tong Wen to Zhao Chen, 2001, published as a co-authored article by Zhao Chen and Tong Wen: Zhao Chen and Tong Wen, "Tong Jun Yu Nanjing De Jianzhu Xueshu Shiye" 童寯与南京的建筑学术事业 [Tong Jun and Architectural Academy in Nanjing], in *Zhongguo Jindai Jianzhu Xueshu Sixiang Yanjiu* 中国近代建筑学术思想研究 *[Research on China's Modern Architectural Academia]*, eds. Zhao Chen and Wu Jiang (Beijing, China: Zhongguo Jianzhu Gongye Chubanshe, 2003), 98.

66. Tong Jun, "Yidai Zheren Jinyiyi, Geng Yu Hechu Mi Zhiyin" 一代哲人今已矣, 更于何处觅知音 [The Philosopher of a Generation Has Passed Away, Where Will I Find Another Who Knew Me so Well], in *Tong Jun Wenji*, 2:311.

67. Han Yu (762–824) was a philosopher and litterateur during the Tang dynasty.

68. David R. Knechtges, "The Prose Works of Han Yu" in ed. Ian P. McGreal, *Great Literature of the Eastern World* (London, United Kingdom: HarperCollins Publishers, 1996), 88–91.

69. Tong Linsu 童林夙, "Shenqie Huainian Wode Fuqin Tong Jun" 深切怀念我的父亲童寯 [Sorely Missed My Father Tong Jun] in *Guanyu Tong Jun*, 121.

70. Su Jun, 苏浚, "Jimin Ouji" 鸡鸣偶记 [Notes in the Early Morning] in *Shuo Fu* 说郛 *[Collections of Notes]* (China: s.n, 1646), 4:126.

71. Zhu Bin 朱彬 (1896–1971) was an alumnus with Tong Jun of Tsinghua University and the University of Pennsylvania. He was also co-founder of Kwan, Chu and Yang Architects (Tianjin and Peiping branches) and the Hong Kong branch of Chu and Yang Architects.

72. Fan Wenzhao 范文照 (1893–1979) was an alumnus with Tong Jun of the University of Pennsylvania. He was also co-founder and the first president of the Shanghai Architectural Society. See Gu Daqing, "Fan Wenzhao Jianzhushi Yu Xianggang Chongji Xueyuan De Xiaoyuan Sheji" in *Shidai Jianzhu* 时代建筑 (2015) 4:168.

73. Zhao Shen 赵深 (1898–1978) was an alumnus with Tong Jun of Tsing Hua College and the University of Pennsylvania. He was also co-founder of The Allied Architects, Shanghai, China. See Zhang Qin 张琴, in Chapter Three of *Fenghuozhong De Huagai Jianzhushi* 烽火中的华盖建筑师 *[Allied Architects at War]* (Shanghai, China: Tongji Daxue Chubanshe 同济大学出版社 Tongji University Press, 2021).

74. Chen Zhi 陈植 (1902–2001) was an alumnus with Tong Jun of Tsing Hua College and the University of Pennsylvania. He was also co-founder of The Allied Architects, Shanghai, China. See Zhang Qin, in Chapter Four of *Fenghuozhong De Huagai Jianzhushi*.

75. Lin Huiyin 林徽因 (1904–1955) was China's first female architect, architectural educationalist, and a famed poet. See Wilma Fairbank, Liang and Lin: *Partners in Exploring China's Architectural Past* (Philadelphia, United States: University of Pennsylvania Press, 1994).

76. Chen Zhi, "Xueguan Zhongxi, Yeji Gonghui–Yi Yanglao Renhui, Tonglao Boqian" 学贯中西, 业绩共辉 —— 忆杨老仁辉、童老伯潜 [Knowledgeable in Eastern and Western Learnings, Brilliant in Careers–In Memory of Yang and Tong] in *Jianzhushi*, 1991, 40:31.

77. "Chinese Student Yang Tingbao Graduates from the University of Pennsylvania with Special Honors, Completing Degree Requirements in Architecture in Less than Three Years," *Philadelphia Evening Bulletin*, February 9, 1925; collected from the University Archives, University of Pennsylvania, United States.

78. *American Exercises in Architectural Designs*, 1927, collected from the Fine Arts School Archives, University of Pennsylvania, United States.

79. Tong Jun, "Yidai Zheren Jinyiyi, Geng Yu Hechu Mi Zhiyin."

80. The War of Resistance refers to the Second Sino-Japanese War that went on from 1937 to 1945.

81. Liberation refers to the founding of the communist People's Republic of China in 1949.

82. Tong Jun, "Wenge Cailiao" 文革材料 [Documents During the Cultural Revolution] in *Tong Jun Wenji*, 4:407.

83. Tong Jun, "Dui Nangong Jianzhu Yanjiushi De Pipan" 对南工建筑研究所的批判 [Critique of the Architecture Research Group of Nanjing Institute of Technology], in *Tong Jun Wenji*, 4:399.

84. Liu Guanghua 刘光华 , *Lieri Zhixia* 烈日之下 *[Life Under the Scorching Sun]*, unpublished, http://id.lib.harvard.edu/alma/990119135280203941/catalog.

85. Liu Guanghua (1918–2018) was a professor at Nanjing Institute of Technology and a colleague of Tong Jun.

86. Fang Yong 方 拥 , "Yinyi De Zhizhe: Jianzhu Dashi Tong Jun De Zuihou Sanshi Nian" 隐逸的智者: 建筑大师童寯的最后三十年 [The Wise Recluse—The Last Thirty Years of Architect Tong Jun], lecture at Banceng Bookstore 半层书店 , Shanghai, China, August 19, 2017.

87. Tong Wen, personal correspondence with the author, 2017.

88. Tong Jun, "Yidai Zheren Jinyiyi, Geng Yu Hechu Mi Zhiyin."

89. Zhao Chen and Tong Wen, "Tong Jun Yu Nanjing De Jianzhu Xueshu Shiye."

90. Tong Linsu, "Shenqie Huainian Wode Fuqin Tong Jun," 121.

91. Tong Jun, *Tong Jun Watercolor Album* [*Tong Jun Shuicaihua Xuan* 童 寯 水 彩 画 选] (Beijing, China: Zhongguo Jianzhu Gongye Chubanshe, 1981).

92. Tong Jun 童寯 , *Tong Jun Sketch Album* [*Tong Jun Sumiao Xuan* 童寯素描选] (Beijing, China: Zhongguo Jianzhu Gongye Chubanshe, 1981).

93. Chen Zhi 陈植 , "Yijing Gaoyi, Caihua Hengyi" 意境高逸, 才华横溢 [Sublime and Lofty Artistic Conception with Brilliant Talents] in *Guanyu Tong Jun*, 17.

94. Ed. Yu Jianhua 俞剑华 , *Zhongguo Meishujia Renming Cidian* 中国美术家人名辞典 *[A Biographic Dictionary of Chinese Artists]*, (Shanghai,China: Shanghai Renmin Meishu Chubanshe [Shanghai People's Fine Arts Publishing House, 1981), 1088.

95. Tong Wen, personal correspondence with the author, 2015.

96. Chen Zhi 陈植, "Yijing Gaoyi, Caihua Hengyi" 意境高逸，才华横溢 [Sublime and Lofty Artistic Conception with Brilliant Talents] in *Guanyu Tong Jun*, 18.

97. Lai Delin 赖德霖, "Tong Jun De Zhiye Renzhi, Ziwo Rentong Ji Xiandaixing Zhuiqiu" 童寯的职业认知，自我认同及现代性追求 [Tong Jun's Career Cognition, Self-Identification and Modernity Pursuit], in *Zheshi: Tong Jun Huaji* 赭石：童寯画纪 *[Sienna—Tung Chuin Grand Tour Diaries]*, ed. Tong Ming (Nanjing: Dongnan Daxue Chubanshe, 2012), 472.

98. Tong Jun's painting on June 12, 1978.

99. Tong Wen, personal correspondence with the author, 2015.

100. Yang Yongsheng, "Jianzhushi Cuican Xinghe Zhong De Juxing—Tong Jun" 建筑师璀璨星河中的巨星——童寯 [The Shining Star of the Architects Galaxy—Tong Jun], in *Guanyu Tong Jun*, 95.

101. Wilma Fairbank, "Laixin" 来信 [Letters], in *Tong Jun Wenji*, 4:484, and Tong Wen's personal correspondence with the author in 2015.

102. Tong Jun, "Foreword," *Tong Jun Watercolor Album*.

103. Tong Jun, *Tong Jun Sketch Album*.

104. Tong Jun, "Zhi Tong Yan Xin" 致童岩信 [A Letter to Tong Yan], in *Tong Jun Wenji*, 4:424.

105. Tong Jun, *Tongjun Jianzhuhua* 童寯建筑画 (Tianjin, China: Tianjin Kexue Jishu Chubanshe [Tianjin Science and Technology Press], 1995).

106. Wu Liangyong, "Tong Jun Jiaoshou De Jianzhuhua" 童寯教授的建筑画 [Architectural Paintings of Tong Jun] in *Guanyu Tong Jun*, 22.

107. Tong Wen, personal correspondence with the author, 2015.

108. Wang Shu, 2012 Pritzker Architecture Prize Laureate acceptance note, The Pritzker Architecture, https://www.pritzkerprize.com/cn/node/957.

109. Zhang Bo 张镈, *Wo De Jianzhu Chuangzuo Daolu* 我的建筑创作道路 *[My Architectural Journey]* (Tianjin, China: Tianjin Daxue Chubanshe 天津大学出版社 Tianjin University Press, 2011).

110. Tong Jun, *Zheshi: Tong Jun Huaji.*

111. Tong Jun, *Zheshi: Tong Jun Hualu* 赭石：童寯画录 *[Sienna—Tung Chuin Grand Tour Painting]*, ed. Tong Ming (Nanjing: Dongnan Daxue Chubanshe, 2012).

112. Tong Ming 童明, "Zheshi" 赭石 [Sienna] in Tong Jun, *Zheshi: Tong Jun Huaji*, 5.

195

113. Liang Sicheng 梁思成, "China's Oldest Wooden Structure" in *Liang Sicheng Quanji* 梁思成全集 *[The Complete Works of Liang Sicheng]* (Beijing, China: Zhongguo Jianzhu Gongye Chubanshe, 2001), 3:361–364.

114. Liang Sicheng 梁思成, "Five Early Chinese Pagodas" in *Liang Sicheng Guanji*, 3:369–372, first published in *Asia Magazine* in August, 1941.

115. Zhao Chen and Tong Wen, "Tong Jun Yu Nanjing De Jianzhu Xueshu Shiye."

116. Liang Sicheng 梁思成, "Zhi Dongbei Daxue Jianzhuxi Diyiban Biyesheng Xin" 致东北大学建筑系第一班毕业生信 [A Letter to the Inaugural Class of Graduates in the Architecture Department at Northeast University] in *Jianzhu Baijia Shuxinji* 建筑百家书信集 *[Letter Collections of 100 Architects]*, ed. Yang Yongsheng (Beijing, China: Zhongguo Jianzhu Gongye Chubanshe, 2000).

117. Tong Shibai 童诗白, "Huiyi Yu Huainian" 回忆与怀念 [Reflection and Remembrance] in *Guanyu Tong Jun*, 105.

118. Liang Sicheng, "Zhi Dongbei Daxue Jianzhuxi Diyiban Biyesheng Xin."

119. Tong Jun, "Zhi Wilma Xin," 4:428. "Phila." is Philadelphia where University of Pennsylvania is located.

120. The Warlord Era in the Republic of China refers to a period (1916–1927) when there was no central government and the country was broken into regions following the collapse of the Qing dynasty, with each ruled by a local leader. The 1911 Xinhai Revolution, which eventually ended the Qing dynasty, brought about the rise of two well-known warlords—Beiyang Army commander Yuan Shikai in the north who had strong military clout, and nationalist Sun Yixian in the south. Manchurian warlords here are Zhang Zuolin and Zhang's son Zhang Xueliang.

121. Tong Jun, "Zhi Wilma Xin," 4:429.

122. Tong Wen, personal correspondence with the author, 2015.

123. Chiang Kai-shek 蒋介石 (1887–1975) was a Chinese nationalist politician and military leader from 1928 to 1975. See Jeremy E. Taylor, "Chiang Kai-shek," Oxford Bibliographies, last modified May 24, 2018, doi: 10.1093/OBO/9780199920082-0119.

124. Tong Wen, personal correspondence with the author, 2015.

125. Tong Jun, *Modern and Contemporary Japanese Architecture* [Riben Jinxiandai Jianzhu 日本近现代建筑] (Beijing: Zhongguo Jianzhu Gongye Chubanshe, 1983).

126. Liang Sicheng, "Laixin" 来信 [Letters] in *Tong Jun Wenji*, 4:438.

127. ibid. 4:443.

128. Wilma Fairbank, "Laixin," 4:489.

129. Tong Wen, personal correspondence with the author, 2017.

130. ibid.

131. Seven intellectuals in Shanghai were arrested in 1936 by Chiang Kai-shek's government. See Sha Qianli 沙千里, *Qiren Zhiyu* 七人之狱 *[Seven Literati Imprisoned]* (Beijing, China: Sheng Huo, Du Shu, Xin Zhi San Lian Shu Dian 生活读书新知三联书店 SDX Joint Publishing, 1984).

132. Printed by Shanghai People's Political Consultative Conference. See also Jiang Ping 姜平, "Jujiao Wang Zaoshi Zuihou Ershinian" 聚焦王造时最后二十年 [Focus on the Last Twenty Years of Wang Zaoshi] in *Duzhe Wenzhai: Wenshiban* 读者文摘: 文史版 *[Readers: Literature & History Edition]* (2015) 2:35–39; First printed at *Wenhui Bao* 文汇报 *[Wenhui Daily]*, May 21, 1957.

133. Zhou Enlai was the first premier (head of government) of the People's Republic of China who served under Chairman Mao.

134. Xin Ziling 辛子陵, *Hongtaiyang de Yunluo: Qiangu Gongzui Mao Zedong* 红太阳的陨落: 千古功罪毛泽东 *[The Crash of the Red Sun: The Eternal Achivements and Crimes of Mao Zedong]* (Hongkong: Shuzuo Fang 书作坊, 2007), 120.

135. See *Maozedong Xuanji* 毛泽东选集 *[Selected Works of Mao Zedong]* (Beijing: Renmin Chubanshe 人民出版社 People's Publishing House, 1977), 5.

136. Zhang Chunqiao was a Chinese political theorist, writer, and politician, and a member of the ultra-Maoist group dubbed the "Gang of Four 四人帮."

137. Chang Shu 常孰, "Zhiwen Peng Wenying" 质问彭文应 [Interrogate Peng Wenying], *Jiefang Ribao* 解放日报 *[Liberation Daily]*, July 19, 1957.

138. See *Maozedong Xuanji*.

139. The anti-Rightist campaign was launched around 1957 by Mao Zedong. It wrongly persecuted and killed many people including prominent intellectuals who were designated as Rightists. See Yen-lin Chung, "The Witch-Hunting Vanguard: The Central Secretariat's Roles and Activities in the Anti-Rightist Campaign" in *The China Quarterly* (Cambridge: Cambridge University Press, 2011), 206:391–411.

140. Sun Dayu, letter to Tong Jun, offered by Tong Jun's family.

141. Zhang Bojun 章伯钧 (1895–1969) was a Chinese politician and intellectual who was declared a Rightist and removed from his ministerial position.

142. Chu Anping (born 1909) was a Chinese scholar and liberal journalist who graduated from the English department of Kwang Hua University 光华大学 in Shanghai. He was also the editor of publications that included *Guancha* 观察 *[The Observer], China Democratic League*—a newspaper targeted at intellectuals—and *Guangming Daily* 光明日报 .

143. Chen Renbing was an intellectual who was personally criticized by Mao Zedong. See Jeanette F. Ford, *Mao's Prey: The History of Chen Renbing, Liberal Intellectual* (Routledge Library Editions) (United Kingdom: Routledge Publishing, 2001).

144. Yan Zuyou 严祖佑 (1943–2022), *Renqu* 人曲 *[Humane Comedy]* (Shanghai, China: Dongfang Chuban Zhongxin 东方出版中心 Orient Publishing Center, 2012).

145. Yan Zuyou, "Jiaoshou Fenggu-Yuyou Sun Dayu" 教授风骨——狱友孙大雨 Professor's Integrity–Cellmate Sun Dayu, in *Shanghai Caifeng* 上海采风 *Shanghai Wave*, November 24, 2014, https://mp.weixin.qq.com/s/PRiywlYZecnZyvG0BOjuIg.

146. Wang Di 王迪, " Ninde Rensheng Shi Zeimeihaode-Fang Kexuejia, Shiren Gao Shiqi" 您的人生是最美好的——访科学家、诗人高士其 [Your Life is the Most Beautiful–Interview with Scientist and Poet Gao Shiqi], in *Beijing Evening News* 北京晚报 , March 29, 1962.

147. Gao Shiqi 高士其 , "Wei Haizimen Xiezuo De Jingguo" 为孩子们写作的经过 [The Course of Writing for Children], in *Wo He Ertong Wenxue* 我和儿童文学 *[I with the Children's Literature]* (Beijing, China: Shaonian Ertong Chubanshe 少年儿童出版社 Juvenile & Children's Publishing House, 1980), 91.

148. Hu Yaobang was one of the main leaders responsible for reassessing the fates of people who had been persecuted, and a promoter of reform and opening up. He was elected as the Communist Party's secretary general in 1980 but was forced to resign in 1987.

149. The Gang of Four 四人帮 refers to a Maoist political faction and was made up of four Chinese Community Party officials: Wang Hongwen 王洪文 , Jiang Qing 江青 , Zhang Chunqiao 张春桥 , Yao Wenyuan 姚文元 .

150. Tong Linsu, "Shenqie Huainian Wode Fuqin Tong Jun," 119.

151. Famous Abraham Lincoln's saying, but no definite source, see David B. Parker, "'You Can Fool All the People': Did Lincoln Say It?," https://historynewsnetwork.org/article/161924.

152. The highest and final degree in the imperial examination (also known as the Metropolitan Exam) in Imperial China.

153. Sir Banister Fletcher, *A History of Architecture on the Comparative Method* (London, United Kingdom: Batsford Books, 1905).

154. Shanhaiguan Pass, also known as Shanhai Pass, is one of the major passes in the great Wall of China.

155. Tong Wen, personal correspondence with the author, 2017.

156. ibid.

157. Tong Linsu, personal correspondence with the author, 2017.

158. Tong Jun, "Wenge Cailiao," 4:376.

159. The Cultural Revolution, known formally as the Great Proletarian Cultural Revolution, was launched in 1966 by Mao Zedong and ended after Mao's death in 1976. See Roderick MacFarquhar, *Mao's Last Revolution* (Massachusetts, United States: Belknap Press of Harvard University Press, 2006).

160. Cultural Revolution self-criticism document offered by Tong Jun's family, 2017.

161. Documents offered by Tong Jun's family, 2017.

162. These were terms used during the Cultural Revolution to demonize people thought to be enemies, and especially favored by Mao Zedong, who used them often to refer to "class enemies."

163. The Three Old Articles or Lao Sanpian 老三篇 referred to political essays said to represent the essence of Mao's ideologies, which extolled selflessness, hard work, and internationalism. See Tan Xuexi, *Lao San Pian De Tihui* (Hongkong: Xianggang Sanlian Shudian 香港三联书店 Joint Publishing HK, 1966).

164. *Zhong zi wu* or Loyalty Dance is a collective dance that became prevalent during the Cultural Revolution. The dancers, grasping the "little red book," (featuring quotations from Chairman Mao), would dance, leap, and shout to the impassioned ring of the music—all to express their boundless loyalty to Mao. See Roderick MacFarquhar, *Mao's Last Revolution.*

165. Tong Jun, "Wenge cailiao," 4:420–421.

166. Tong Wen, personal correspondence with the author, 2017.

167. The Four Olds or the Four Old Things referred to pre-communist elements of Chinese culture: old ideas, old culture, old customs, and old habits.

168. Tong Linsu, "Shenqie Huainian Wode Fuqin Tong Jun," 119.

169. ibid.

170. Tong Jun's manuscript collected by his family.

171. Mao Zedong 毛泽东 , *Mao Zedong Xuanji* 毛泽东选集 [Selected Works of Mao Tse-Tung(Zedong)], (Beijing: Renmin chubanshe, 1951).

172. Tong Wen, personal correspondence with the author, 2017.

173. Liu Guanghua, *Lieri Zhixia*.

174. ibid.

175. ibid.

176. "Hong Bao Shu" 红宝书 [Red Treasury Book] were quotations from Chairman Mao Zedong—an icon of China and communism—as well as a work of propaganda, often wrapped in its distinctive vinyl cover. During China's Culture Revolution, it became virtually mandatory to own and carry one. See Yu Hongli 余红俐, "Cong Jundui Dao Minjian: Wenge Qianzhongqi De Hong Bao Shu Jiqi Chuanbo" 从军队到民间："文革"前中期的"红宝书"及其传播 [From the Army to the Society: the Red Treasury Books and Their Propagation], in *Dangshi Bolan* 党史博览 *[Extensive Readings of CCP History]* (2017), 1:24–27.

177. Stephen Hawking, "Galileo Galilei," in *On the Shoulders of Giants* (Philadelphia, United States: Running Press, 2002), 393.

178. Tong Jun, "Wenge Cailiao," 4:419.

179. Don Quixote is the main character in a Spanish novel titled *The Ingenious Gentleman Don Quixote of La Mancha*.

180. Tong Wen, personal correspondence with the author, 2017.

181. Xie Junmei 谢俊美, "Luelun Sun Zhongshan Jindai Minzu Guojia Sixiang De Xingcheng" 略论孙中山近代民族国家思想的形成 [On Sun Yatsen's Formation of Modern National State Thought], in *Lishi Jiaoxue Wenti* 历史教学问题 *[History Research and Teaching]* (2016), 3:24–33.

182. Ni Zan was a Chinese painter from the Yuan dynasty and during the early Ming period.

183. Tong Jun, "Wenge Cailiao" 文革材料 [Documents During the Cultural Revolution] in *Tong Jun Wenji*, 4:419.

184. Tong Wen, personal correspondence with the author, 2017.

185. Tong Linsu, personal correspondence with the author, 2017.

186. Li Shangyin 李商隐 (813–858), poem "Yeyu Jibei" 夜雨寄北 [Note to the North on Raining Night], in *Li Shangyin* (New York, United States: New York Review Books, 2018).

187. From *Xinan Yincao* 西南吟草 *[Poetry Drafts in Southwest]*, an anthology of poetry by Tong Jun and his friends during 1930s–1940s, unpublished.

188. Tong Wen, personal correspondence with the author, 2017.

189. Tong Shibai 童诗白, "Huiyi Yu Huainian" 回忆与怀念 [Reflection and Remembrance] in *Guanyu Tong Jun*, 104.

190. Tong Jun, personal correspondence with Tong Linsu.

191. Tong Wen, personal correspondence with the author, 2017.

192. ibid.

193. ibid.

194. ibid.

195. ibid.

196. ibid.

197. The house was designed in 1935 by renowned American architect Frank Lloyd Wright in southwest Pennsylvania, United States. It was designated as a national historic landmark; accessed September 26, 2022, https://fallingwater.org.

198. Wang Xizhi (303–361) was a famous calligrapher during the Jin dynasty. See "Wang Xizhi," Britannica online, Biography, https://www.britannica.com/biography/Wang-Xizhi.

199. Tong Wen, personal correspondence with the author, 2017.

200. ibid.

201. *Xinan Yincao* 西南吟草 *[Poetry Drafts in Southwest]*, an anthology of poetry by Tong Jun and his friends, written in the 1930s–1940s, but never published.

202. ibid.

203. Chen Zhi 陈植 , "Yijing Gaoyi, Caihua Hengyi," in *Guanyu Tong Jun*, 16.

204. Tong Jun's Cultural Revolution self-criticism document offered by Tong Jun's family, 2017.

205. Shanghai Dianying Xitong "Banye Jijiao" Bianshezu 上海电影系统 "半夜鸡叫" 编摄组 , ed., *Banye Jijiao* 半夜鸡叫 *[The Cock Crows at Midnight]* (Shanghai, China: Shanghai Renmin Chubanshe 上海人民出版社 Shanghai People's Publishing House, 1970).

206. Gao Yubao 高玉宝 , *Banye Jijiao* 半夜鸡叫 *[The Cock Crows at Midnight]* (Beijing, China: Waiwen Chubanshe 外文出版社 , 1973).

207. Referring to *hong haiyang*, when the large walls of streets and work units were painted red in 1966, building momentum for exaggerating Mao Zedong's authority. See Jin Yucheng 金宇澄 , ed., *Piaobo Zai Hong Haiyang: Wode Dachuanlian* 漂泊在红海洋: 我的大串联 *[Drifting in the Red Ocean: My Revolutionary Tours]* (Taipei, Taiwan: Shibao Wenhua Chuban Qiye Youxian Gongsi 时报文化出版企业有限公司 China Times Publishing Co., 1996).

208. Zhu Shunshui 朱舜水 (1600–1682) remained loyal to the Ming dynasty after its demise. In 1659, he settled down in Japan and gave lectures to Tokugawa Mitsukuni. He had a direct impact on the Meiji Restoration and the prosperity that followed. See "Zhu Shunshui," Biography, Britannica online, https://www.britannica.com/biography/Zhu-Shunshui.

209. Ji Cheng 计成 (1582–1642), *Yuan Ye* 园冶 *[Craft of Gardens]*, ed. Liu Yanchun 刘艳春 (Nanjing, China : Jiangsu Fenghuang Wenyi Chubanshe 江苏凤凰文艺出版社 Jiangsu Phoenix Literature and Art Publishing Ltd., 2015). This book is currently considered by many to be the first monograph dedicated to garden design in the world.

210. Inaba Kunzan Hen, ed., *Shu Shunsui Zenshū* 朱舜水全集 *[The Completed Works of Zhu Shunshui]* (Tokyo, Japan: Bunkaidō, 1912).

211. Ma Yuan 马援 (14 BCE – 49 CE), "Ma Yuan Jie Xiongzi Yan Dun Shu" 马援诫兄子严敦书 [Ma Yuan Admonishes His Brother's Sons Ma Yan and Ma Dun] in *Guwen Guanzhi*; this is a letter from Ma Yuan to his elder brother's sons, Ma Yan and Ma Dun, to warn them to discipline themselves in society.

212. Li Bai 李白 (701–762), "Chunye Yan Taoliyuan Xu" 春夜宴桃李园序 [Preface to "A Banquet in Taoli Garden"], in *Guwen Guanzhi*; the poem illustrates the poet's understanding of life through the description of a feast.

213. Liu Yuxi 刘禹锡 (772–842), "Loushi Ming" 陋室铭 [Epitaph on a Lowly Hut], in *Guwen Guanzhi*.

214. Kong Zi 孔子 (551–479 BCE), *Lun Yu* 论语 , *[The Analects]*—the most important, and most influential classic of Confucianism in Chinese history.

215. Lao Zi 老子 (571–471 BCE) was the author of *Daode Jing* 道德经 *[The Tao Te Ching]*, one of the classics of Taoism.

216. Zhuang Zi 庄子 (c. 369–286 BCE) was the author of *Zhuangzi* 庄子 [Chuang-tzu], the most important book on Taoism on par with *Daode Jing*.

217. Jean-Paul Sartre (1905–1980) was a French playwright, novelist, screenwriter, political activist, biographer, and one of the leading figures in the philosophy of existentialism (and phenomenology). See Christian Skirke, "Jean-Paul Sartre," Oxford Bibliographies, last modified April 28, 2014, doi. org.10.1093/OBO/9780195396577-0192.

218. Immanuel Kant (1724–1804) was a German philosopher, and one of the central Enlightenment thinkers. See Lara Denis, "Immanuel Kant: Ethics," Oxford Bibliographies, last modified September 30, 2013, doi: 10.1093/OBO/9780195396577-0225.

219. Zhuang Zi 庄子, "Paoding Jieniu" 庖丁解牛 [The Dexterous Butcher], in *Zhuangzi* 庄子 [Chuang-tzu]. The fable demonstrates the importance of spotting rationales and following rules by dissecting cows.

220. *Yi Jing* 易经 was the most important piece of literature in ancient China. It demonstrates the relationship between life and the universe by describing changes in things. Later generations often use it for fortune-telling.

221. Tong Wen, "Yi Zufu de Liangjian Xiaoshi" 忆祖父的两件小事, in *Guanyu Tong Jun*, 129.

222. Tong Wen, personal correspondence with the author, 2017.

223. Tong Shibai 童诗白, "Huiyi Yu Huainian" 回忆与怀念 [Reflection and Remembrance] in *Guanyu Tong Jun*, 106.

224. Liu Zhiping, a letter to Tong Jun.

225. Zhu Qiqian 朱启钤 (1872–1964) served as the minister of transportation for five terms and the minister of internal affairs for three terms, and was the acting prime minister of the Beiyang Government. He founded the first Central Park in Beijing, the first Cultural Heritage Exhibition Hall in China, and the Society for Research in Chinese Architecture. See Beijingshi Zhengxie Wenshi Ziliao Yanjiu Weiyuanhui and Zhonggong Hebeisheng Qinhuangdao Shiwei Tongzhanbu, ed., *Huogong Jishi: Zhu Qiqian Xiansheng Shengping Jishi* 蠖公纪事：朱启钤先生生平纪实 *[Chronicle of Zhu Qiqian]* (Beijing, China: Zhongguo Wenshi Chubanshe, 1991).

226. *Zhongguo Yingzao Xueshe Huikan* 中国营造学社汇刊 *[Bulletin of The Society For Research in Chinese Architecture]* was the journal of the Society for Research in Chinese Architecture (SRCA), with a total of seven volumes, twenty-three issues, and twenty-two volumes published from 1930 to 1945 that discuss, among other articles, the important work conducted by the society.

227. Liang Sicheng 梁思成, *Qingshi Yingzao Zeli* 清式营造则例 *[Ch'ing Structural Regulations]* (Beijing, China: Qinghua Daxue Chubanshe, 2006).

228. Li Jie 李诫 (1035–1110), *Yingzao Fashi* 营造法式 *[Song Manual Building Standards]* (Beijing: Zhongguo Shudian, 2006); was an official work on rules of Chinese architecture written by Li Jie in 1100 and published in 1103 by the Song Dynasty Court.

229. Liang Sicheng, "Laixin" 来信 [Letters], in *Tong Jun Wenji*, 4:436.

230. This was the conflict between Chinese and Japanese troops near the Marco Polo Bridge (Lugouqiao) outside Beiping (July 7, 1937), which developed into warfare in Far East Asia as the prelude to the Pacific part

of World War II. See "Marco Polo Bridge Incident," Britannica online, last updated February 18, 2023, https://www.britannica.com/event/Marco-Polo-Bridge-Incident.

231. Tong Jun, "The Manchu Garden," in *Tong Jun Wenji*, 1:75.

232. Zhu Qiqian 朱启钤, "Laixin" 来信 [Letters], in *Tong Jun Wenji*, 4:441.

233. Liang Sicheng, "Laixin," 4:443.

234. Liu Dunzhen 刘敦桢, "Xu" 序 [Foreword], in Tong Jun 童寯, *Jiangnan Yuanlin Zhi* 江南园林志 *[On Classical Gardens in Southeastern China]*, 1.

235. "Shelun: Kaizhan Baijia Zhengming, Fanrong Jianzhu Chuangzuo" 社论：开展百家争鸣，繁荣建筑创作 [Let All Schools Speak out and Architectural Creativity Flourish], in *Jianzhu Xuebao* 建筑学报 *[Architecture Journal]* (Beijing, China: Zhongguo Gongye Chubanshe, 1961), 3:1.

236. Liu Dunzhen, in Tong Jun, *Jiangnan Yuanlin Zhi*, 2.

237. Zhao Chen 赵辰 and Tong Wen 童文, "Tong Jun Yu Nanjing De Jianzhu Xueshu Shiye" 童寯与南京的建筑学术事业 [Tong Jun and Architectural Academy in Nanjing], in *Zhongguo Jindai Jianzhu Xueshu Sixiang Yanjiu* 中国近代建筑学术思想研究 *[Research on China's Modern Architectural Academia]*. See also note 65.

238. Tong Jun 童寯, "Zhuzhe Yuanxu" 著者原序 [Preface], in *Jiangnan Yuanlin Zhi*, 4.

239. Tong Jun 童寯, "Zaoyuan" 造园 [Gardening], in *Jiangnan Yuanlin Zhi*, 8.

240. Wang Guowei, "Renjian Cihua" 人间词话 [Poetic Remarks on the Human World], in *Wang Guowei Wenji*, 1:147.

241. Yang Xuanzhi 杨衒之, *Luoyang Qielan Ji* 洛阳伽蓝记 *[Luoyang Temples before the Raid]* (Beijing, China: Zhonghua Shuju 中华书局 Zhonghua Book Company, 2007). This is a record of Buddhist monasteries in Luoyang.

242. Yang Yongsheng 杨永生, "Jianzhushi Cuican Xinghezhong De Juxing—Tong Jun" 建筑师璀璨星河中的巨星——童寯 [The Shining Star of the Architects Galaxy—Tong Jun] in *Guanyu Tong Jun*, 95.

243. Wang Shu 王澍, "Zhiyou Qingqu" 只有情趣 [Just for Pleasure], in *Dongnan Yuanshu*, 5–14.

244. Yang Yongsheng, "Jianzhushi Cuican Xinghezhong De Juxing—Tong Jun."

245. Liu Dunzhen 刘敦桢, *Suzhou Gudian Yuanlin* 苏州古典园林 *[Classical Gardens of Suzhou]*.

246. Tong Wen, personal correspondence with the author, 2017.

247. Liu Xujie, personal correspondence with the author, 2017.

248. Tong Jun 童寯, "Dui Nangong Jianzhu Yanjiushi De Pipan" 对南工建筑研究室的批判 [Critique of the Architecture Research Group of Nanjing Institute of Technology], in *Tong Jun Wenji*, 4:399.

249. Liu Xujie, personal correspondence with the author, 2017.

250. Tong Wen, personal correspondence with the author, 2017.

251. Qin Lei 秦蕾, editor of the Tongji University Press.

CHRONICLE OF TONG JUN'S LIFE

10.02.1900 – Tong Jun was born in Dongtaizi Village near Mukden (present-day Shenyang). His original family name was Niohuru, and he was from the Manchu Plain Blue Banner, one of the Eight Banners of Manchu military and society during the Qing dynasty.

1901 – The Qing Empire signed the Boxer Protocol.

1903 – Tong Jun's younger brother Tong Yin was born.

1904–1905 – The Russo-Japanese War broke out.

1905 – The whole family moved to Shenyang and lodged with Tong Jun's father's student, Ka.

1906 – Tong Jun went to kindergarten. His younger brother Tong Cun was born.

1908 – Tong Jun entered the Mukden "Mengyang Yuan" (Qing-style kindergarten). His younger brother Tong Yan was born.

09.1910 – Tong Jun entered the Mukden No.1 Provincial Elementary School (Public Exemplary Elementary School). He started to study English and graduated in 1914.

10.1910–04.1911– A plague broke out in northeast China. Tong Jun's youngest brother Tong Yan passed away from the pandemic. Tong Jun and Tong Yin took shelter temporarily in a temple.

1911 – Hsinhai Revolution ended the Manchu-led Qing dynasty. Tong Jun felt upset when he saw flags with "Elevate the Han and Exterminate the Manchus" written on them. He did not cut off his braid until three years later.

07.1914 – World War I broke out.

09.1917 – Tong Jun entered the Mukden No.1 Middle School. He subscribed to *English Weekly* and the *English Journal* published in Shanghai. He practiced speaking English at the Aiwen English School in downtown Shenyang during holidays, which was established by a British expatriate, and often listened to English lectures on science and art at the YMCA. He started to practice oil painting and pencil sketching.

11.1918 – World War I ended.

1919 – Tong Jun married Guan Weiran. The May Fourth Movement and the New Culture Movement broke out.

02.1920 – Tong Jun's first son Tong Shibai was born.

1921 – After graduating from middle school, Tong Jun participated in the entrance exams of Tangshan Chiao Tung University and Beiping Tsing Hua College, ranking first and the third respectively among all the candidates. In September, Tong Jun entered Tsing Hua College.

1923–1925 – Tong Jun joined the Fine Arts Society of Tsing Hua and associated with members of the society, including Wen Yiduo, Liang Sicheng, and Zhang Zhizhong. With the help of Miss Starr and Miss Gauthier, he achieved significant progress in pen drawing and watercolor painting and held his own solo art exhibition. He served as the art editor for the *Tsinghua Yearbook*.

09.1925 – After graduating from Tsing Hua College, Tong Jun studied in the Architectural Department at the University of Pennsylvania (UPenn) in the United States. Under the guidance of his design tutor George Howard Bickley, he took part in several architectural design competitions with fruitful outcomes: his designs of the Rodin Museum in 1927 and the Protestant Church in 1928 won the second prize and the first prize, respectively, of the Arthur Spayd Brooke Memorial Prize. Under the guidance of the watercolor painter George Walter Dawson, Tong Jun improved his painting skills and held his solo art exhibition. He was a member of the Chinese Students' Alliance of America and the Tsing Hua Alumni Association.

1928 – Tong Jun graduated with a master's degree. He was a member of the Architectural Society at the University of Pennsylvania and the T Square Society.

06.1928–04.1930 – Tong Jun worked as an architect in the U.S. for Ralph B. Bencker in Philadelphia and then for Ely Jacques Kahn in New York.

05.1930–08.1930 – Tong Jun took his Grand Tour of Europe, passing through the United Kingdom, France, Germany, Italy, Switzerland, Belgium, and the Netherlands, returning to China by way of Eastern Europe and the Soviet Union. He completed quite a few paintings during this time and witnessed achievements of the modern architectural movement.

09.1930 – Tong Jun took up the position of professor in the Architecture Department at Northeastern University in Shenyang at the invitation of Sun Guofeng, the president of the School of Engineering, Northeastern University. While serving as a professor, he completed a variety of essays including "Five Architectural Orders," "Various Forms of Domes," "Drawing Notes and Architectural Terms," "Guide for Techniques," "Proportion," and "Twin Tower

Temple in Peking" (published by *Chinese Architecture*, 1931), and compiled architectural textbooks.

06.1931 – Tong Jun served as the chairman of the Architecture Department at Northeastern University. After the Japanese troops took over Shenyang during the September 18 Incident (also known as the Mukden Incident), he helped his students escape and later he lived in Beijing in exile.

1931 – Tong Jun published an essay titled "A Brief History of the Architecture Department at Northeastern University" in *Chinese Architecture*, issue 1, 1931. He became a member of the Tsing Hua Alumni Association in Shanghai. In November, Tong Jun went to Shanghai at the invitation of Chen Zhi to establish The Allied Architects with Chen Zhi and Zhao Shen. The Allied Architects (co-founded in 1932) later became the largest private architectural office in China with around 200 architectural designs completed. Tong Jun himself served as the board member of the China Architects Association and a member of the Xi Society.

1932 – Tong Jun's mother passed away from illness. Tong Jun started to survey and research gardens around Shanghai. Tong Jun co-founds The Allied Architects with Chen Zhi and Zhao Shen. He also contributed his spare time to teaching the exiled senior students from Northeastern University.

1933 – Tong Jun's second son, Tong Linsu was born. Tong Jun became a member of the China Architects Society of Shanghai and served as the board member.

1934 – Tong Jun translated the article "Vitruvius on the Education of Architects," which was published in *Chinese Architecture*, volume 2, issue 8, 1934.

1936 – Tong Jun published the article "Chinese Gardens, Especially in Jiangsu and Zhejiang" in *T'ien Hsia Monthly* in October.

1937 – After the Marco Polo Bridge Incident on July 7, the Second Sino-Japanese War broke out. In August, the Battle of Shanghai erupted. By November, the majority of Shanghai was taken over by Japanese troops.

1937 – Tong Jun published the articles "Manchu Garden" and "Architecture Chronicle" in *T'ien Hsia Monthly*, October 1937. He completed the manuscript for *Jiangnan Yuanlin Zhi (On Classical Gardens in Southeastern China)*.

05.1938 – Tong Jun was invited to Chongqing to design architecture in southwest China. He designed military factories for the National Resources Commission—including Zizhong alcohol factory, a copper smelter, and an ironwork factory. He published the article "Foreign Influence in Chinese Architecture" in *T'ien Hsia Monthly*, May 1938; the article was also included in *Chinese Houses and Gardens* by Henry Inn, edited by Shao Chang Lee and published by Honolulu Fong Inn's Limited in 1940 (pages 17–22), together with his article, "Chinese Gardens: Contrasts; Designs" (pages 23–29).

end of 1939–beginning of 1940 – During his short stay in Shanghai, Tong Jun participated in the study of the book *Chinese Culture Series* and took charge of the compilation of Chinese painting history and Chinese garden design. He completed "Timber Frame Tradition" and "Chinese Culture Series," which remained unpublished.

1940 – Tong Jun traveled to Chongqing and Guiyang in spring to establish a subsidiary architectural office and design school buildings, science museums, exhibition halls, and other such venues.

1941 – Tong Jun published the essay "Characteristics of Chinese Architecture" in the journal *Zhanguoce*, issue 8, 1941.

autumn of 1944 – Tong Jun served as a professor in the Department of Architecture at Central University in Chongqing at the invitation of the chairman Liu Dunzhen. He wrote the articles "Architectural Education" and "Vogues in Ancient China," which remained unpublished.

1945 – Tong Jun's father passed away.

1946 – After the Second Sino-Japanese War came to an end, Tong Jun came back to Shanghai and soon moved to Nanjing to oversee the projects of The Allied Architects. Meanwhile, he also served as a professor at National Central University. He published "A Review of the Appearance of Public Buildings in China" in *Gonggong Gongchen Zhuankan*, 1946.

1947 – Tong Shibai went to the U.S. to further his education.

1948 – Tong Jun became a member of the Chinese Institute of Engineers.

1950 – Tong Jun co-founded The Allied Architects & Engineers and stayed in National Central University after it was renamed Nanjing University. He was later engaged in long-term mandatory political studies to reform his ideology and accept criticism.

1952 – The Allied Architects & Engineers was shut down. After Nanjing University evolved into Nanjing Institute of Technology, Tong Jun continued his teaching career. He served as a member of the Chinese People's Political Consultative Conference (CPPCC) Jiangsu Committee and was People's Congress deputy of Jiangsu Province in 1964. He was a member and board member of the Architectural Society of China.

1955 – Tong Jun's firstborn son, Tong Shibai, came back from the U.S. to teach at Tsinghua University with his wife Zheng Min who taught in Beijing Normal University. His second son, Tong Linsu, graduated from Peking University and joined the navy. Tong Jun was infected with acute meningitis during an academic trip to Beijing, which put him in a coma for nearly ten months.

1956 – Tong Jun's wife Guan Weiran passed away. Tong Linsu moved to Nanjing to live with Tong Jun, during which time Tong Linsu assumed a teaching "position in the Department of Electronic Engineering at Nanjing Institute of Technology" and undertook scientific research on electron display.

1958 – Tong Jun was in the Bourgeois Intellectual Teacher Ideological Reform Study Group at Nanjing Institute of Technology, listening to denouncements and writing ideological reports after six days of labor.

1963 – Tong Jun worked at the Third Research Studio in the Architecture Department in autumn and had a surgery due to cancer in November. *Jiangnan Yuanlin Zhi* was published.

1964 – Tong Jun returned to the university (Nanjing Institute of Technology) and resumed work in May. He took a year's leave beginning in July, during which he gave a series of lectures titled "An Overview of the Renaissance in Europe," "European Classics," and "A History of Modern Western Architecture," and returned to the Third Research Studio in September 1965.

1964 – Tong Jun published the article "Pavilion," in *Nangong Xuebao*, issue 1.

1966 – The Cultural Revolution started. Tong Jun was forced to join the "Ruziniu" study group. He was put through struggle sessions and forced labor, during which his salary was held and his property was confiscated.

1968 – Tong Jun's grandson Tong Ming was born.

1976 – The Cultural Revolution ended.

1979 – Liu Dunzhen's *Classical Gardens of Suzhou* was published by Zhongguo Jianzhu Gongye Chubanshe (China Architecture & Building Press); in 1979, and later its English edition was published by SDX Joint Publishing in Hong Kong; Tong Jun wrote the preface.

1980 – A series of works of Tong Jun were published: "Western Buildings in the Eternal Spring Garden in Beijing" was published in *Architects*, issue 2; "New Architecture and Genres" was published by China Architecture & Building Press; "Research on the Suiyuan Garden" was published in *Architects*, issue 3; the "Complete Process of the Construction of the Sydney Opera House" was published in *Architects*, issue 4; and "A History of Foreign Memorial Buildings" was published in *Architects*, issue 5.

1981 – The article "Pedigree of New Architecture" was published in *Architects*, issue 5; "An Account on Architectural Design Scheme Competitions" was published in *Architects*, issue 7, and "Baroque and Rococo" was published in *Architects*, issue 9. The books *Selected Watercolor Paintings of Tong Jun* and *Selected Sketches of Tong Jun* were published.

1982 – The article "History of Architectural Technologies" was published in *Architects*, issues 10, 11, 12, and 14. *Architecture of the Soviet Union* was published by China Architecture & Building Press. Tong Jun completed the manuscript for *Dongnan Yuanshu (Glimpses of Gardens in Eastern China)*, and the articles "History of Architectural Education" and "Modern Architecture of Eastern Europe."

03.1983 – Tong Jun passed away in Nanjing. *History of Garden Construction* and *Modern Architecture of Japan* were published by China Architecture & Building Press. The article "The Impact of Chinese Gardens on the East and the West" was published in *Architects*, issue 16.

— FAMILY TREE —

17th generation   18th generation   19th generation

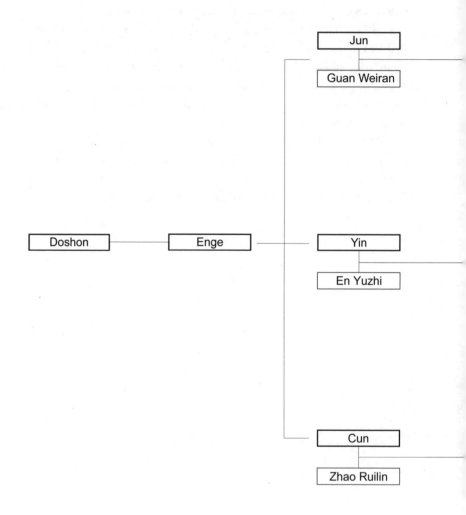

213

— LIST OF KEY INDIVIDUALS —

Chapter One

Xiang Bingren (1944–) started his architectural study in 1961 and graduated from the Department of Architecture at Nanjing Institute of Technology in 1966. After several years of working in Anhui Province as an architect, he went back to the university and got his master's degree in 1981 and PhD degree in 1985, respectively, after which he worked several years in the U.S. and Hong Kong. He founded DDB International Ltd. (later named DDB Architects) in Shanghai and became a professor in the Architecture and Urban Planning College at Tongji University in 1999. His published works include *Frank Lloyd Wright* and the Chinese translation of *The Image of the City* by Kevin Lynch.

Fang Yong studied in the Department of Architecture at Nanjing Institute of Technology from 1977 to 1982 and became a postgraduate student of Tong Jun. He started his career as a faculty member in the Department of Architecture of Huaqiao University in Quanzhou, Fujian, upon graduating in 1984 and became a professor in the Center for Architecture Research, Peking University, in 2001. His published works include *Gucheng Quanzhou* [*Ancient City Quanzhou*].

Tong Wen (1962–), son of Tong Jun's second son, Tong Linsu, is a wireless communications scientist. He graduated from the radio engineering department at the Nanjing Institute of Technology in 1984 (now School of Information Science and Engineering at Southeast University), and received his PhD degree in Canada. He had been engaged in the research of wireless communications technologies at Nortel, Canada, since 1994 before becoming the chief scientist on wireless communications at Huawei in 2009. He has more than 500 awarded U.S. patents (1G-6G wireless) and numerous awards in recognition of his innovations in wireless technologies.

Tong Cun (Tsun Tung; 1906–1994), the second younger brother of Tong Jun, was a microbiologist and medical scientist. He was a pioneer in the discipline of antibiotics in China, finding the People's Republic's very own penicillin, and later also discovering erythromycin. After graduating from Yenching University Prepatory School with a Doctorate in Medicine and Philosophy, he started working and teaching in Peking Union Medical College Hospital. He went to Johns Hopkins University in 1940, and started his research on penicillin in the National Epidemic Prevention Station after returning to China in 1945. He served as the director of the Penicillin Laboratory of the East China People's Pharmaceutical Company from 1949, widely recognized in China as "the father of penicillin," following his successful synthesis of the antibiotic and commercialization. He also conducted research on the breeding of penicillium, streptomycetaceae, and streptomyces aureofaciens, as well as the trial production of chlortetracycline.

Zhan Yongwei was a student of Tong Jun and a middle school classmate of his third son Tong Linbi. He was a researcher on Professor Liu Dunzhen's *Classical Gardens of Suzhou* and chief engineer of Suzhou Gardening and Greening Bureau. He graduated from the Department of Architecture, Nanjing Institute of Technology in 1959, and undertook part of the painting and writing of *Classical Gardens of Suzhou.*

Tong Linbi (1935–2022), the third son of Tong Jun, was an expert on space electronics for the defense industry. After graduating from the radio engineering department at the Nanjing Institute of Technology in 1958, he worked for No. 743 People's Liberation Army from 1960 to 1965, then in the Division Five Institute for the Ministry of National Defense of the People's Republic of China.

Wilma Fairbank (1909–2002), the author of *Liang and Lin, Partners in Exploring China's Architectural Past* was a historian of Chinese art. She graduated from the Department of Art History at Radcliffe College in the U.S. in 1931 and left for China in 1932. In 1942, she started working in the China section of the State Department's cultural relations division and was later appointed cultural attaché to the United States Embassy in China in 1945. Two years later, she returned to the U.S. in pursuit of a career in academic studies and writing.

Liang Sicheng (Ssu-cheng Liang; 1901–1972) was a schoolmate of Tong Jun in Tsing Hua College and the University of Pennsylvania in the U.S. He was an architectural historian and an architectural educator. He studied in Tsing Hua College (later University) from 1915 to 1923 and entered the Architecture Department at the University of Pennsylvania in 1924. He received his master's degree in 1927, after which he stayed briefly at Harvard University to study further. In 1928, he went back to China and founded the Department of Architecture at Northeastern University. He later joined the Society for Research in Chinese Architecture in 1931, spending decades surveying and studying historic architecture. He founded the Architecture Department at Tsinghua University from 1946 to 1947. His works include *A Pictorial History of Chinese Architecture.*

Qi Kang (1931–) graduated from the Department of Architecture at Nanjing University (later Nanjing Institute of Technology) in 1952. He has served as the associate chairman and chairman in the Department of Architecture, as well as vice president. His works include *Enlightenment of Architecture.*

Yan Longyu was an assistant of Tong Jun during the 1980s and former chief editor of Southeast University Press.

Tanaka Tan (1946–2012) graduated from Yokohama National University and the University of Tokyo respectively in1969 and 1971. He was a Professor Emeritus of Kyoto University whose research focused on the history of Chinese architecture and landscape gardens.

Guo Husheng (1931–2008) was a professor at Southeast University (previously Nanjing Institute of Technology) and chief editor of *The History of Architectural Technology.* He graduated from the Architecture Department at Nanjing University (later Nanjing Institute of Technology) in 1952.

Liu Guanghua (1918–2018) was the author of *Beijing: The Cornucopia of Classical Chinese Architecture*, Chinese Architecture and *Under the Scorching Sun.* He studied in the Architecture Department at National Central University from 1936 to 1940 and became a faculty member. In 1946, he attained his Master of Architecture from Columbia University in the U.S. and became a professor in the Architecture Department at National Central University (which was later restructured to form Nanjing University and the Nanjing Institute of Technology) in 1947.

Zhong Xunzheng (1929–2023) graduated from the Department of Architecture at Nanjing University (later Nanjing Institute of Technology). He taught at Hunan University and Wuhan University successively before taking up a position at Nanjing Institute of Technology (now Southeast University).

Yang Tingbao (Ting Pao Yang; 1901–1982) was a schoolmate of Tong Jun at Tsing Hua College and the University of Pennsylvania in the U.S. He completed a bachelors in 1924 and a masters in 1925 in the Architecture Department at UPenn, then returned to China in 1927. He joined Kwan, Chu & Yang Architects, soon becoming a prominent architect. After 1949, he served as the vice-governor of Jiangsu Province, the vice-president and president of the Chinese Architects Society, the vice-president of the International Union of Architects. He was a professor at National Central University from 1940s and the chairman of the architecture department.

Wang Tingfang was a son of Tong Jun's close friend and a doctor at the Nanjing General Hospital for Defence.

Tong Linsu (1933–2020) was the second son of Tong Jun and a professor at Southeast University. After graduating from Peking University in July 1955, he joined the staff of the Dalian Naval Base, conducting nuclear physics and nuclear energy research. In 1957, he started teaching in the School of Electrical Engineering at the Nanjing Institute of Technology, where he researched the physics of the electronic beam and its applications. He was also responsible for and led the commercialization and mass production of color television sets in China.

Tong Wei (1956–), the daughter of Tong Jun's eldest son Tong Shibai, is a poet and painter. Her published works include *Horse Head Turning Back* in 1988.

Chapter Two

Huang Yiluan was Secretary of Party Branch of the School of Architecture at Southeast University from 1980 to 1986.

Zhu Guangya (1942–) was a professor at Southeast University. His areas of expertise include the preservation and research of architectural heritage.

Wang Shu (1964–) is a professor at China Academy of Art. He was a winner of the Pritzker Architecture Prize. He studied in School of Architecture at Southeast University from 1981 to 1988 and took up teaching at China Academy of Art upon graduation. He got his PhD degree from Tongji University in 2000 and founded Amateur Architecture Studio in collaboration with Lu Wenyu.

Yang Yongsheng (1931–2012) was a publisher of architecture books and former chief editor of *Architect*, as well as former deputy managing editor of China Architecture & Building Press.

Liu Dunzhen (Liu Tun-Tseng; 1897–1968) was an architectural historian and educationalist and chief editor of *Classical Gardens of Suzhou*. He went to Japan in 1913 and enrolled in the Mechanical Engineering

Department at the National Institute of Technology, Tokyo College, in 1916 and transferred to the Architecture Department the following year. In 1922, he returned to China and founded Huahai Architectural Firm with Liu Shiying. He contributed to the creation of the architecture department at Suzhou Industrial Specialized School in 1923, and the Department of Architecture at National Fourth Sun Yat-sen University (later National Central University) in 1927. In 1933, he assumed the position of full-time researcher and chair of the literature department in the Society for Research in Chinese Architecture, focusing on the study of traditional Chinese architecture. He became a professor and chairman of the Architecture Department at National Central University in 1943.

Yuan Yiwei was a botanical researcher at Nanjing Botanical Garden.

Chapter Three

Liang Qichao (1873–1929), father of Liang Sicheng, was a prominent politician, educationalist, thinker, litterateur, and historian in modern China.

Wang Guowei (1877–1927) was a Chinese philosopher, educationalist, thinker, litterateur, historian, and aesthete. He joined Dongwen Xueshe founded by Luo Zhenyu in 1898. In December 1900, he entered the Tokyo Academy of Physics in Japan and returned to China the following year. He then served as a translator and teacher in Wuchang Agricultural College and was editorial writer and deputy chief editor of *Education World*. Later, he taught in Nantong Normal College and Jiangsu Normal College before his sojourn in Japan after 1911. In 1923, he acted as *nanshufang xingzou* (a literary attendant in the South Chamber) to serve the abdicated emperor, Puyi. In 1924, he started teaching in Tsing Hua College. He drowned himself in the Summer Palace, leaving behind substantial works of vast varieties.

Zhao Yuanren (Yuan-Ren Chao; 1892–1982) was a Chinese modern linguist and musicologist. He was admitted to the preparatory course of Nanjing Jiangnan Higher School in 1907 and went to Cornell University in the U.S. to study mathematics, earning his bachelor's degree in 1914. After graduation, he studied philosophy, first in the graduate school at Cornell, and then in Harvard the following year, getting his PhD degree in philosophy in 1918. He taught physics as a lecturer at Cornell University in 1919, went back to China and taught physics and psychology at Tsing Hua College in

1920, taught philosophy and Chinese at Harvard University from 1921 to 1924, became a tutor of the Tsinghua Academy of Chinese Learning and a professor in their Philosophy Department, and took up the role of researcher and head of the Linguistics Department in the Institute of History and Philology, Academia Sinica (China), from 1929 to 1938. From then on, he successively taught at Yale University, Harvard University, the University of Michigan, and the University of California, Berkeley. In 1945, he was elected the president of the Linguistic Society of America.

Chen Yinque (Yin-Koh Tschen; 1890–1969) was a Chinese educationalist, linguist, litterateur, historian, and poet. He received his education from Siyi School founded by his father from an early age and later went to Japan to further his education with his older brother. In 1907, he went to Fudan Public School in Wusong and studied successively at Humboldt University of Berlin (Germany), University of Zurich (Switzerland), University of Paris (France), and Harvard University, but all without a diploma. In 1925, he returned to China and became a professor at Tsing Hua College before the war broke out, during which he taught at National Southwestern Associated University (China), Hongkong University, Guangxi University, and Yenching University. He came back to Tsinghua University in 1946 and started teaching in Lingnan University and Sun Yat-sen University from 1949. He was criticized during the Cultural Revolution and tortured to death.

Wang Wenxian (J. Quincey Wong; 1886–1968) was an educationalist and dramatist. He came back to China after graduating from London University in the U.K. in 1915, before which he served as the Chinese Commissioner of Treasury in Europe. He became an English professor at Tsing Hua College in 1921 and acted as the vice-president and deputy president. In 1927, he went to Yale University in the U.S. to study screenwriting under Professor George Pierce Baker, during which he wrote *She Stoops to Compromise* and *Peking Politics*, both performed on stage at Yale University in 1927 and 1929 respectively. He came back to Tsinghua University in the following year to teach foreign drama and modern drama. He was elected chairman of the Foreign Literature Department. In 1937, he became a professor at St. John's University in China. After the Second Sino-Japanese War, he went to Hong Kong and later migrated to the U.S.

Mei Yiqi (Yi-chi Mei; 1889–1962) was an educationalist, hailed as "the President of Tsinghua University forever." He was sent to the U.S. as one of the Boxer Indemnity Scholarship Program students in 1910 and studied at Worcester Polytechnic Institute. After graduating in 1914, he took up posts as a teacher, a professor in the Physics Department, and was dean of Tsing Hua College, later becoming president of Tsinghua University in 1931. From 1937 to 1945, he set up the Southwest Associated University where he worked during the Second Sino-Japanese War. After the war ended, he resumed the position as the president of Tsinghua University. In 1950, he worked at the China Institute in New York City. In 1955, he founded the Tsinghua Institute of Atomic Science in Hsinchu, Taiwan. In 1958, he was appointed Ministry of Education of Taiwan and concurrently served as president of Taiwan National Tsing Hua University.

Bing Zhi (1886–1965) was a zoologist and major founder of modern biology in China. He graduated from the Imperial University of Peking and earned his bachelor and PhD degrees from Cornell University in 1913 and 1918 respectively. After returning to China in 1920, he served as a professor at Nanjing Normal College, Southeast University, Xiamen University and was dean of the Biology Department at National Central University. He established China's first biology department in 1921, and in 1922, co-founded the China Biological Laboratory of Science Society, the first biology research institute in China. He taught at Fudan University from 1949.

John Ma (1882–1966), the pioneer educationalist in P.E. graduated from St. John's University in 1911 and went to Springfield College (United States) to study P.E. twice, first from 1919 to 1920 and later from 1925 to 1926. He taught in Tsing Hua College/Tsinghua University from 1914 to 1966.

Hu Shi (Shih Hu; 1891–1962) was a thinker, litterateur, philosopher, and one of the most influential and controversial scholars in modern China. He started studying at Cornell University in 1910 and Columbia University (U.S.) in 1915. In 1917, he became a professor at Peking University. From 1938 to 1942, he served as the ambassador of the Republic of China to the U.S. He then served as the president of Peking University in 1946 and left for the U.S. in 1949. In 1952, he was a member of the International Commission for a *History of the Scientific and Cultural Development of Mankind* (a series by UNESCO) and returned to Taiwan in the same year to give lectures. In 1957, he became the president of the Academia Sinica.

Tong Shibai (1920–2005), the eldest son of Tong Jun, was a major founder of electronics studies in China. He graduated from Hangchow University in 1942, earned his Bachelor of Electrical Engineering at the

National Southwestern Associated University (China), and taught in the Electrical Engineering Department at Tsinghua University after graduation. From 1948 to 1951, he studied at the Electrical Engineering Department at Illinois State University (U.S.), attaining his master's in 1949 and PhD in 1951. He served as a lecturer and associate professor with the Electrical Engineering Department at Polytechnic Institute of Brooklyn (U.S.) from 1952 to 1955. He came back to China in 1955 and became a professor at Tsinghua University.

Zheng Min (1920–2022), wife of Tong Shibai, Tong Jun's eldest son, was a poet and poetry critic. She graduated from the philosophy department of National Southwestern Associated University in 1943 and got her Master in English Literature from Brown University (U.S.) in 1952. In 1955, she went back to China and took up the study of English literature in the Literature Research Institute at Chinese Academy of social Sciences, and also taught in the Foreign Languages Department at Beijing Normal University in 1960. She resumed writing poems in 1979.

Tong Lang (1962–), son of Tong Jun's eldest son, Tong Shibai, is a professor at Cornell University. He earned his Bachelor of Science in Automation from Tsinghua University in 1985, Master of Science in Electrical Engineering in1988, and PhD in electrical and communications engineering from the University of Notre Dame in 1990. He completed his postdoctoral studies at Stanford University (U.S.) in 1991. He joined Cornell University in 1998, where he is now the Irwin and Joan Jacobs Professor in Engineering and the Cornell site director of the Power Systems Engineering Research Center (PSerc).

Wen Yiduo (1899–1946) was a poet and scholar. He achieved major accomplishments in new Chinese poetry, the promotion of the new form and rhythm of poetry, and classical Chinese literature and traditional culture. He studied at Tsing Hua College from 1912 to 1921 and attended the Art Institute of Chicago and University of Colorado and New York Academy of Art successively after leaving for the U.S. in July 1922. He served as the dean of the National Art School in Peiping (now Beijing) after traveling back to China in May 1925. He then took up posts as a professor at the National Fourth Sun Yat-sen University (later renamed the National Central University), Wuhan University, Qingdao University, the National Art School in Peiping, National Chengchi University, Tsinghua University, and National Southwestern Associated University. He was assassinated after publishing *The Last Speech*.

Wen Yiqi (1903–1956), younger brother of Wen Yiduo, was a poet and doctor. He was the first to translate *The Theory of Relativity* by Einstein into Chinese while he was in Tsing Hua College. He got his Bachelor in Medicine School in 1926 and Doctor of Medicine in 1930 from The University of Chicago, after which he worked as a physician in Michael Reese Hospital. In 1931, he returned to China and became the chief of medicine at the Central Hospital of Nanjing. He founded his own clinic in Hankou in 1932. During the Second Sino-Japanese War, he practiced medicine in Chongqing and returned to Hankou in 1946. After 1949, he served as the chief of medicine at the Second Hospital of Wuhan, and a consultant at the Hankou Union Hospital.

Liang Shiqiu (Shih-chiu Liang; 1903–1987) was a literary critic, prose writer, translator, and educator. He entered Tsing Hua College in 1915, went to the U.S. to study English and Western literature in August 1923, and earned his PhD from the English Department at Harvard University. From 1926, he taught successively at National Southeastern University (later renamed the National Central University and Nanjing University), Qingdao University (later renamed National Shandong University) and Beijing Normal University. In 1927, he founded the Crescent Moon Society along with Xu Zhimo and Wen Yiduo. He spent some time in Sichuan during the Second Sino-Japanese War and migrated to Taiwan in 1949, after which he took the positions of director of the National Institute for Compilation and Translation, chairman of the English Department at the Provincial Normal College of Taiwan, and dean of the Literature School at National Taiwan Normal University, and was also a member of the board of Tatung University.

Chen Zhi (Benjamin Chih Chen; 1902–2002) was a schoolmate of Tong Jun at both Tsing Hua College and the University of Pennsylvania, and an architect and architectural educationalist. He studied at Tsing Hua College from 1915 to 1923 and entered the Architecture Department at the University of Pennsylvania upon graduation. He traveled back to China in 1929 and taught at Northeast University and co-founded Liang, Chen, Tong & Cai Architects and Engineers. In 1932, he, Zhao Shen, and Tong Jun founded The Allied Architects, one of the most influential architectural offices in modern China. In 1938, he set up the architecture department at Hangchow University. He was also among the founders of the East China Design & Research Institute (the predecessor of East China Design & Research Institute Co. Ltd) when it was first established in 1952. In June 1955, he was appointed the deputy director and chief architect of the Shanghai Urban Planning and Architecture Administration, and later became the director and chief architect of the Shanghai Civil Architectural Design Institute in 1957.

Huang Jiahua (1903–1988) was an architect and architectural educationalist. He left for the U.S. upon graduation from Tsing Hua College and earned two master's degrees from the Massachusetts Institute of Technology (MIT) in the U.S. After returning to China, he took a position in Shanghai East Asian Architecture Company and went on to be the first chairman of the Architecture Department at University of Shanghai. He founded the architecture department at Chongqing University, serving as the chairman. During the war, he served as a professor in both the architecture departments at Chongqing University and the National Central University. After the war ended, he became a professor in the Architecture Department at Hangchow University. After 1949, he served successively as a professor at Hangchow University, an architect at The Allied Architects & Engineers, and a professor at Tongji University.

Cai Fangyin (1901–1963) was a civil engineering expert, architectural educationalist, and inventor of the Chinese character 砼 , which stands for concrete. He got his Bachelor in Civil Engineering from MIT in 1927 and his master's in 1928. In 1930, he went back to China and served as a professor at Northeast University, as well as a professor and the chairman of the Civil Engineering Department at Tsinghua University (including the period when it was merged into the National Southwestern Associated University). He was also the chairman of the Civil Engineering Department and then dean of the School of Engineering at National Chung Cheng University. In 1946, he wrote and compiled the first textbook on structural mechanics in China titled *General Mechanics*. He took positions as a member in the government committee of the Jiangxi Provincial Government & Culture and Education Committee, and as dean of the School of Engineering at Nanchang University. From 1951 to 1953, he was appointed chief engineer of the Ordnance Bureau of the Heavy Industries Ministry and later became the vice-president and chief engineer of China Academy of Building Research, Ministry of Architectural Engineering, from 1956 to 1963.

Lin Tongji (Tung-chi Lin; 1906–1980) was a political scientist and expert on Shakespeare studies. He left for the U.S. after graduating from Tsing Hua College to study international relations and Western literary history at the University of Michigan in 1926, earning his bachelor's degree in 1928. He got his master's in 1930 and PhD in 1933 in political science from the University of California, Berkeley. He worked as a lecturer at the University of California and Mills College in Oakland from 1930 to 1932, teaching Chinese literary history. He returned to China in 1934 and started teaching at Nankai University. He served as the dean of the Literature School at Yunnan University from 1937 to 1943, and a professor of comparative politics at Fudan University from 1942 to 1945, during which time he co-founded the journal *Zhan Guo Ce (Warring States Strategies)*. He became a professor of English and Western literature at Fudan University in 1945. He was labeled a Rightist in 1958. In 1980, he was invited to the U.S. to give lectures, but he passed away from a heart attack while at the University of California.

Guo Yuanxi (Yuan Hsi Kuo; 1905–1966) was an architect. He worked on completing his bachelor's degree from the Architecture Department at the University of Pennsylvania from 1926 to 1929 and got his master's from MIT in 1930, after which he took a position as professor at the Peiyang Institute of Technology. He then went to the U.S. in 1933 to supervise the construction of the China Pavilion in the Chicago World's Fair, imitating the Golden Pavilion in Rehe. In 1936, he started teaching at SoengKen University of Canton and worked as an architect for Wang Kuancheng in Hong Kong since 1949.

Ha Xiongwen (Harris Wayne Ha; 1907–1981) was an architect and an expert on urban planning and urban construction management. He graduated from Tsing Hua College in 1927 and from the Architecture Department at the University of Pennsylvania in 1932. He served as the director of the Department of Architecture at the University of Shanghai and was also a professor there. He was also the director of the Construction Department in the Ministry of Civil Affairs of the Kuomintang Government. After 1949, he took positions as a professor in Fudan University, Jiaotong University, Tongji University, Harbin Institute of Technology, and the Harbin Institute of Architecture and Engineering successively.

Liang Yan (Yen Liang; 1908–2001) was a Chinese American architect and designer. He first immigrated to the United States in 1928 to continue his architectural studies at Yale, MIT, and Cornell. In 1932, he secured a position in the first group of apprentices selected to study with the experimental Taliesin Fellowship under Frank Lloyd Wright. Liang later returned to China for eleven years and enjoyed a successful architectural practice. During the war, he served with the U.S. Army in China, even designing a home for a top military official. In the late 1940s, Liang returned once again to the U.S., working briefly at Taliesin before taking the position as chief designer at the New York firm of Harrison & Abramovitz. There, he contributed designs to the United Nations' buildings and the striking First Presbyterian Church of Stamford, Connecticut (affectionately known as "Fish Church;" https://www.fishchurch.org/Sanctuary-Panorama), among many others. In addition to architectural pursuits, Liang also wrote and illustrated children's books, including a sweet story from 1958 called *The Skyscraper*. After retiring from architecture, he moved to California and worked in ceramics, made music, and designed furniture.

Wang Huabin (Huapin Pearson Wang; 1907–1988) was an architect and architectural educationalist. He left for the U.S. in 1927 upon graduating from Tsing Hua College, and studied in Oberlin College and the University of Pennsylvania before getting his master's degree. In 1933, he returned to China, working first for the Office of Architects, Shanghai Central District Construction Committee, and then for Dong Dayou Architectural Office. From 1937 to 1948, he was a professor at Shanghai University and Hangchow University, and served as the first chairman of the Architecture Department at Hangchow University. In 1945, he was appointed chief architect for Shanghai Central Trust. He served as the chief engineer at the East China Architectural Design & Research Institute, the Beijing Industrial Architecture Design Institute, and the China Academy of Building Research from 1952.

Huang Xueshi was born in Qingjiang, Guangxi Province. He graduated from Tsing Hua College in 1926 and earned his master's degree in civil engineering from MIT and worked as a professor at the School of Engineering of National Chung Cheng University after the Second Sino-Japanese War. After the foundation of the PRC, he first taught in the Civil Engineering Department at Nanchang University, and was thereafter transferred to the Infrastructure Project Supervision Division of Huazhong Institute of Technology and Zhongnan Construction Engineering School to take the post as director. After 1958, he took the position of deputy chairman and later chairman of the Civil Engineering Department at Hunan University. In his later years, he served as a consultant and senior engineer for the Institute of Architectural Economics and China Academy of Building Research, and was a member of the Research Group on Architectural Economics of International Council for Building Research Studies and Documentation.

Zhang Zhizhong was a professor and chairman of the Architecture Department at Nanjing Institute of Technology.

Wu Liangyong (1922–) is an expert in architecture and urban planning. He graduated from the Architecture Department at the National Central University in 1933, entered the Architecture and Urban Design Department at Cranbrook Academy of Art (U.S.) in 1948 and got his master's degree in 1950. He then went back to China and taught in the Architecture Department at Tsinghua University. In 1978, he became chairman of the Architecture Department at Tsinghua University.

Dai Nianci (1920–1991) studied at the Architecture Department at National Central University from 1938 to 1942 and stayed on as a teaching assistant after getting his bachelor's degree. From 1944 to 1948, he worked as an architect in the Chongqing and Shanghai branches of Xingye Architectural Office. He made contributions to the construction of a socialist China, serving as the chief engineer and chief architect of the Central Architectural Construction Design Institute. He was also the deputy director of the Ministry of Urban and Rural Development and Environmental Protection, and the chairman of the Chinese Architects Society. The principles of being "applicable, economical and aesthetic," which he proposed, were officially adopted as the guidelines of national civil constructions by the Chinese central government.

Lin Zhu (1928–), ex-wife of the architectural scholar Cheng Yingquan, was the wife of Liang Sicheng after Ling Huiyin's death. She worked first as the secretary and later the librarian in the Architecture Department at Tsinghua University.

Chapter Four

Su Jun (1542–1599) was a famed expert on neo-Confucianism during the late Ming dynasty. His works include *Yijing Ershuo, Sishu Ershuo,* and *Weibian Weiyan.*

Zhu Bin (Pin Chu; 1896–1971) went to Tsing Hua College in 1914, entered the University of Pennsylvania (U.S.) in 1918, and earned his master's degree in 1922. In 1924, he and Guan Songsheng founded Kwan, Chu & Yang Architects (Tianjin and Peiping branches). In 1949, he founded the Hong Kong branch.

Fan Wenzhao (Robert Fan; 1893–1979) graduated from the Civil Engineering Department at St. John's University in 1917. After working at St. John's as an engineering professor for two years, he pursued a bachelor's degree in architecture from the University of Pennsylvania from 1919 to 1922. In 1927, he founded his own architectural office and initiated the Architectural Society of Shanghai China, with Zhuang Jun and Lv Yanzhi, as the first president. He moved to Hong Kong after 1949.

Zhao Shen (Shen Chao; 1898–1978) went to Tsing Hua College in 1911 and entered the Architecture Department at the University of Pennvania in 1920 and earned his master's degree in 1923. In 1930, he set up Shen Chao Architects, which was later merged into Chao & Chen Architects in collaboration with Chen Zhi in February 1931. With Tong Jun joining them in 1931, it later evolved into The Allied Architects in 1932. From 1950 to 1952, he co-founded The Allied Architects & Engineers. In 1952, he served as the chief engineer at East China Architectural Design Co. Ltd. From 1953 to 1955, he took the position of chief engineer at the Central Design Company of China, Department of Construction Engineering, and became the deputy director and chief architect of East China Architectural Design Co. Ltd. in 1956. He is famed for representative works of his office including the Shanghai YCMA, Nanking Theater, Railway Administration Hall, the Ministry of Foreign Affairs building in Nanjing, Metropol Theater, National Commercial Bank, Maoxin Flour Mill in Wuxi, Wuxi Shenxin No. 3 Textile Factory, and Jiangnan University.

Lin Huiyin (Phyllis Whei-yin Lin; 1904–1955), China's first female architect, was an architectural educationalist in modern China and a poet. She went to the School of Fine Arts at the University of Pennsylvania in 1924 and earned her Bachelor of Fine Arts, after which she studied stage design at Yale University (U.S.). She was also long engaged in the study of Chinese architectural heritages. She participated in the design of the National Emblem of the People's Republic of China, the Monument to the People's Heroes, and the revival of Chinese cloisonné.

Guan Songsheng (Sung-sing Kwan; 1892–1960) attended St. John's University in 1911 and was later admitted to Tsing Hua College. He had a passion for sports and went to the Massachusetts Institute of Technology (MIT) in 1914 and got his bachelor's degree in architecture in 1917, after which he studied municipal administration at Harvard University (U.S.) for a year in 1919. After going back to China in 1919, he served successively as consultant on the Tianjin Police Station Project, architect for the Beining Street in Tianjin project, and as a member of the engineering team of the National Capital Reconstruction Commission. In 1920, he established Kwan, Chu & Yang Architects in Tianjin, engaging in projects from all major cities. After he moved to Taiwan in 1949, he took to promoting sports, specifically track and field, and was thus hailed as "the father of track and field in Taiwan."

Zhang Yongsen (Yung-sun Chang; 1909–1983) was editor of *Yingzao Fayuan*. He graduated from the Architecture Department at National Central University in 1931. The positions he held included architect in the Sun Yat-sen's Mausoleum Management Committee, engineer of the National Resources Commission, associate professor at National Central University, professor at Nanjing University, professor and deputy chairman of the Department of Architecture at Nanjing Institute of Technology, and vice-chairman of Jiangsu Standards Institution.

Zhao Chen graduated from the Department of Architecture, Nanjing Institute of Technology. He worked in the university and later became a professor in the School of Architecture and Urban Planning at Nanjing University, engaging in the study of architectural history and theories.

Zhang Yuzhe (1902–1986) was one of the founders of modern Chinese astronomy. In 1919, he gained entrance to Tsing Hua College. In 1923, he studied in the Mechanical Engineering Department at Purdue University (U.S.) and the Architecture Department at Cornell University (U.S.) successively, after which he entered the Astronomy Department at The University of Chicago (U.S.) in 1925. In 1928, he discovered Asteroid No. 1125, which was given the name "China," as the first asteroid discovered by the Chinese. Receiving his PhD from the Astronomy Department at the University of Chicago in 1929, he went back to China and became a professor in the Physics Department at the National Central University. In 1941, he took the position as head of the Astronomy Research Institute at National Central University and served as the director of the Purple Mountain Observatory from 1950 to 1984. In 1978, *Minor Planet Circulars* announced that Asteroid No. 2051 was named "2051 Chang."

Chen Faqing (1901–2004) was the wife of Yang Tingbao. She graduated first from the Beijing Women's Higher Normal School and then the National Art School in Beiping (now Beijing). After marriage, she stayed at home looking after her husband and children.

Chen Jing, wife of Liu Dunzhen, entered the College of Chinese Language and Literature at Hunan University in 1929 and married Liu Dunzhen in 1930, after which she stayed at home looking after her husband and children. In her later years, she and her son Liu Xujie completed a biography of her husband, *In Memory of the Life of Shineng*.

Chapter Five

Tang Dingzhi (Tang Di; 1878–1948), alias Dingzhi was originally named Xiang, which he later changed to Di because of his admiration for Shi Tao, also known as Da Dizi. He was already adept in the calligraphy of Wei Stele, the year he came of age. At the start of the Republic of China, he worked at Suzhou Public Secondary Industrial School, and worked as a secretary for the Ministry of Transportation and the National Audit Office in 1911. In 1914, he taught calligraphy at Peking Women's Normal University and taught painting at the Xuannan Painting Society in 1915. He was hailed as one of the "Four Masters in the North," along with Xiao Qianzhong, Xiao Junxian, and Chen Banding. In 1918, he became a mentor of the Painting Technique Institute at Peking University and taught traditional Chinese painting as a professor at Beijing Art School, during which time he participated in the compilation of the *List of Calligraphic Works and Paintings in the Institute of Antiquity Exhibition*. From 1929 to 1933, he served as a professor at the School of Art, Peking National Specialist Arts School. In 1935, he co-founded the Society of Nine with Xie Yucen, Zhang Shanzi, Zhang Daqian, Zheng Wuchang, Fu Tienian, Xie Gongzhan, Wang Shizi, and Lu Danlin.

Du Shunbao was a professor at Southeast University and chief architect of the Urban Planning & Design Institute of Southeast University. He entered the Nanjing Institute of Technology in 1957. He specializes in the design of classical Chinese gardens, the planning and design of national parks, and restoration design of historic buildings. His representative works include the reconstruction projects of Jiming Temple in Nanjing, Yuejiang Tower, Jinghai Temple and Tianfei Palace, Keyan Scenic Spot, Mudu Scenic Spot of Taihu Lake, and Shajiabang Scenic Area in Changshu. He published *Classical Gardens of China and the Complete Works of Chinese Architectural Art, Volume 19 (Landscape Architecture)*.

Shao Yu, a sketch artist, watercolor artist, publisher, and poet had been obsessed with painting ever since his childhood. In 1934, he studied at Shenyang Fine Arts Specialist School and Peking Fine Arts Specialist School (national schools of fine arts). The positions he held included chief editor of *Jianghai Journal of Central Jiangsu Province*, president of the Central Jiangsu branch of Xinhua News Agency, president and chief editor of People's Fine Arts Publishing House, executive director and secretary of China Artists Association, chairman of the Editing and Publishing Committee of the *Complete Works of Chinese Fine Arts*, and chairman and party secretary of the China Calligraphers Association.

Tong Yan, the nephew of Tong Jun, was an associate professor in the Art School at Renmin University in Beijing. He earned his Bachelor in Fine Arts from Capital Normal University (China) in 1986 and his Master in Fine Arts from the National Higher Institute for Fine Arts Antwerp in Belgium in 1991.

Zhang Bo (1911–1999) gained entrance to Northeastern University (China) in 1930 and later studied in the Civil Engineering Department at Tsinghua University for three months in 1931, later transferring to the Architecture Department at National Central University in Nanjing in 1932. Upon graduating in 1934, he worked in Kwan, Chu & Yang Architects. In 1951, he joined Yong Mao Construction Company after coming back from Hong Kong, and later became the chief architect of the Beijing Institute of Architectural Design & Beijing Municipal Institute of City Planning and Design. He hosted and participated in several major projects such as the Great Hall of the People, the Cultural Palace of Nationalities, Beijing Friendship Hotel, and the Beijing Hotel. He was also the author of *My Career of Architectural Creation*.

Chapter Six

Liu Hongdian (1904–1995) graduated from the Department of Architecture at Northeastern University (China) with a bachelor's degree in 1933. He worked as an architect at the Bank of Communications from 1936 to 1939, and at the headquarters of Zhejiang Commercial Bank from 1939 to 1941. He set up Zongmei Architectural Specialist School in 1941 and founded Dingchuan Architects and Engineers in 1947. He later became a professor at the architecture department of Northeastern University in 1949 and served as the first chairman of the architecture department at Xi'an Institute of Metallurgy and Construction Engineering since 1956. His works included Shanghai Centre Pool, Shanghai Center Library, Bank of Communications in Fuzhou, Bank of Communications in Nantong, Bank of Communications in Hangzhou, the Majestic Building on West Nanjing Road, Shanghai, the campus planning and design of the Metallurgy Building of Northeast Institute of Technology, and classroom buildings of the Chinese Academy of Sciences, Changchun Branch.

Guo Yulin (born 1906) graduated from the Architecture Department at Northeastern University in 1932 and worked as a clerk at The Allied Architects. He was the leader of a drawing division at the Department of Architecture, Bank of China in Shanghai and associate architect at Shanghai Jianming Architects. In August 1938, he became a professor at the Civil Engineering Department at National Northwest Institute of Technology (China) and served as director of the Shaanxi Enterprise Company in 1944. He held the post of chairman of the Architecture Department at Shenyang Institute of Technology from 1949 to 1950, chairman of the Architecture Department at Northeast Institute of Technology from 1950 to 1953, and deputy chairman of the Architecture Department at Northeast Institute of Technology from 1953 to 1956, while at the same time serving as an editor of the *Architectural Journal* since October 1953. In 1956, he was appointed a member of the Shenyang Committee of Urban and Rural Construction. In the same year, the Department of Architecture at Northeast Institute of Technology (including the divisions of architecture, industrial and civil architectural structure, industrial and civil architecture and heating, and gas supply and ventilating) was merged with Xi'an Institute of Metallurgy and Construction Engineering; he then went to Xi'an and served as the curator of the Northeast Institute of Technology's library from 1963 to 1982, and then as dean of Xi'an Institute of Metallurgy and Construction Engineering. From 1965 to February 1966, he held the position of deputy commander in chief of the Headquarter of Infrastructure Construction.

Liu Zhiping (Chih-ping Liu; 1909–1995) was a historic architecture expert and professor. He was among the first class of the Architecture Department at Northeastern University in 1928 and was later transferred to National Central University from which he graduated in 1932. He worked for The Allied Architects in 1933 and served as an architect at the Zhejiang Commission for the Management of Landscape in 1934. He joined the

Society for Research in Chinese Architecture (SRCA) as an assistant in 1935, served as a member of the Historiographical Commission for Chinese Architecture, National Central Museum in 1942, worked as a researcher of the Society for Research in Chinese Architecture in 1943, and held the position of associate professor and then professor in the Architecture Department at Tsinghua University in 1946. His works included *Chinese Building Design Reference Drawing Album* (with Liang Sicheng as the chief editor), *Yi ke yin in Yunnan, Types and Structure of Chinese Architecture, A Brief History of Chinese Residential Buildings—Cities, Houses and Gardens,* and *Chinese Islamic Buildings.*

Zhang Zuolin (1875–1928) was the father of Zhang Xueliang. He spent his early years in poverty and was valued by Zhao Erxun, based on a recommendation from Yuan Jinkai, after years of military service. After 1916, he became the most powerful person in Northeast China, serving successively as superintendent of military affairs in Liaoning and governor-general of the Three Eastern Provinces. Nicknamed "King of Northeast China," he became the leader of the Fengtian Army. In 1927, he held the position of grand marshal of the army and navy of the Republic of China, becoming the last ruler of the Beiyang Government and the most powerful ruler of the whole country of the Republic of China. In 1928, he was mortally wounded by a bomb at Huanggutun and died the same day.

Chiang Kai-shek (Jiang Jieshi, 1887–1975) was a politician of critical importance in modern China. He successively held the position of president of the Whampoa Military Academy, commander-in-chief of the National Revolutionary Army, president of the Nationalist Government, premier of the Executive Yuan, chairman of the Military Affairs Commission, General Special Class of the Republic of China, president of the Kuomintang, chairman of the San Min Chu-i Youth Corps, the highest commander of the allied power in China, and president of the Republic of China. He was the top leader of China from 1928 to 1949.

Zhang Xueliang (Hsueh-liang Chang/Peter H. L. Chang; 1901–2001) was a warlord who in two turbulent weeks in 1936 helped turn the course of Chinese history. He graduated from Fengtian Military Academy in 1920. After his father, Zhang Zuolin, passed away in 1928, he succeeded him as the leader of the Northeast Army. In 1936, he started the Xi'an Incident, after which he was under house arrest for fifty-five years. In 1995, he migrated to the U.S.

Chapter Seven

Wang Zaoshi (1902–1971) entered Tsing Hua College in 1917, left for the U.S. in 1925 and earned his PhD in political science from the University of Wisconsin (U.S.). After returning to China, he served as professor and dean of the literature department at Kwang Hua University and founded journals, including *Advocacy and Criticism* and *Freedom Forum*. In late 1935, he joined the Shanghai Cultural Salvation Council. In November the following year, he was arrested along with Shen Junru and Zou Taofen, and others as one of the "Seven Gentlemen." After he was released, he was elected to the National Political Council, and later founded the *Daily Front* and Shanghai Free Press. He was also a member of the Culture and Education Committee, East China Military and Political Commission. In 1951, he became a professor at Fudan University. He was arrested in 1966 and died in prison in 1971. His works and translations included *The State in Theory and Practice, A History of European Diplomacy, Lectures on the Philosophy of History* and *Absurd Notes*.

Luo Longji (1896–1965) entered Tsing Hua College in 1913 and studied at the University of Wisconsin and Colombia University (U.S.), eventually graduating with a PhD in political science from London School of Economics and Political Science (U.K.). After going back to China in 1928, he was a professor at Kwang Hua University and Nankai University. After 1949, he was appointed as the vice-president of the Revolutionary Committee of Chinese Kuomintang and Minister of Forest Industry. His proposal on "setting up a Commission for Political Rehabilitation" was listed among the Three Right-wing Political Theories. His works included *Human Right Theories, Collection of Political Essays,* and *Refutation Against the US Secretary of State Acheson*.

Peng Wenying (1904–1962) was one of the Three Heroes of Anfu (Jiangxi Province) and one of the Five Rightists (along with Zhang Bojun, Luo Longji, Chu Anping, and Chen Renbing), advocating that "the original rulings of rightist are held and no adjustments shall be made except for removing the label." He entered Tsing Hua College in 1917 and went to the U.S. in 1925, where he earned his bachelor's degree in political science from the University of Wisconsin and his master's degree in political science from Columbia University. In 1932, he came back to China and became a professor at Shanghai University of Law and Kwang Hua University.

Shen Junru (1875–1963) obtained the *jinshi* degree in 1904 and entered Hosei University in Japan in 1905. After going back to China in 1908, he took up teaching and was engaged in politics. He became president of the Supreme People's Court and chairman of the China Democratic League after 1949.

Zhang Naiqi (1897–1977) graduated from Hangzhou Provincial Business School in 1918, after which he worked in Zhejiang Industry Bank. In 1932, he co-founded the China Credit Society. Subsequent positions included professor at Shanghai University and Kwang Hua University, head of the finance department in Anhui Province, and co-founder of the China Democratic National Construction Association. From 1949, he was a member of the Government Administration Council of the Central People's Government, head of Ministry of Food, and the co-founder of the All-China Federation of Industry and Commerce. His published works include *Symposium of Zhang Naiqi* and *Jiliu Collection*.

Zou Taofen (1895–1944) went to St. John's University (China) in 1919, became editor of the journal *Life Weekly* in 1926, and founded the journals *Life of the Masses* and *Life Daily* in 1935 and 1936, respectively. He was arrested and then released along with Shen Junru, Li Gongpu, Sha Qianli, Shi Liang, Zhang Naiqi, and Wang Zaoshi, after which he started the journals of *Kang Zhan, Quanmin Kangzhan,* and *Kangzhan Huabao.*

Li Gongpu (1902–1946) entered Shanghai University in 1925 and studied in the Political Science Department at Reed College in the U.S. In 1932, he published *Shun Pao Monthly* and *Shun Pao Yearbook* in China and founded Shun Pao Afterwork School for Women in 1933. In 1934, he started the journal *Reading Life* and the company Reading Life Press in 1936. He then founded the University of Society in 1946 and was assassinated in the same year. His works include *Enemy's Rear in Northern China—Jin-Cha-Ji, Theory of Nationwide Mobilization, The Road of Youth, Theories and Practices of War of Resistance Education,* and *Shanxi on Its Way to Victory.*

Sha Qianli (1901–1982) entered Shanghai University of Law in 1928 and served as the chief editor of the weekly journal *Qingnian Zhiyou*. He was arrested along with six other people, including Shen Junru, in 1936. In 1939, he founded a few companies such as Founding of the Nation Machine Factory, Jiancheng Shiye Company, Sino-US Soft Drink Factory, and Nanyang Company. After 1949, he served as the vice-secretary of the Central Military Committee of Shanghai, vice-secretary of the Shanghai Municipal

People's Government, vice-minister of Trade of the Central People's Government, vice-minister of Commerce, Minister of Local Industry, Minister of Light Industry, Minister of Food, and the vice-chairperson of the Chinese People's Political Consultative Conference.

Shi Liang (1900–1985) entered Shanghai University of Law and Politics in 1923 and became a lawyer in 1931. She was arrested in 1936 as one of the famed Seven Gentlemen along with Shen Junru, Li Gongpu, Sha Qianli, Zou Taofen, Zhang Naiqi, and Wang Zaoshi. After 1949, she served as the Minister of Justice, vice-president of the All-China Women's Federation, and vice-president of the National Committee of Chinese People's Political Consultative Conference.

Zhou Enlai (1898–1976) was a long-serving top leader of the Communist Party of China. He has made great contributions to the foundation of the People's Republic of China, and he aided Mao Zedong to consolidate the leadership of the Communist Party of China.

Song Qingling (Soong Ching-ling/Rosamond; 1893–1981) left for the U.S. in 1907 and went to a private school in New Jersey, U.S. She got her bachelor's degree in literature from Wesleyan College. In 1914, she worked as Sun Yat-sen's secretary and became his wife in 1915. After Sun Yat-sen passed away in 1924, she remained active in social political activities. After 1949, she held the position of vice-president, and later honorary president of the People's Republic of China, serving as the representative of national image. Before her death, she was admitted to the Communist Party of China.

Tang Enbo (1898–1954) entered the Military Academy of Zhejiang Army in Aid of Fujian in 1919 and went to Japan with Tong Weizi, son of a wealthy businessman in Wuyi, in 1921. He entered the Law Department at Meiji University in 1922 and gained admission to the Japanese Army Academy through the recommendation of Chen Yi, a general of the Kuomintang military, in 1924. After going back to China upon graduation in 1926, he married Wang Jingbai, Chen Yi's foster daughter. He led the fights in the Battle of Taierzhuang, Battle of Xuzhou, and Battle of Wuhan during the Second Sino-Japanese War and was appointed the general of the Republic of China Army.

Zhang Chunqiao (1917–2005) joined the Shanghai chapter of the League of Chinese Left-Wing Writers in 1936 and joined the Chinese Communist Party around 1940. He served as deputy director of the East China branch of the New China News Agency (1950), managing director of *PLA Daily* (1954), and was a member of the Shanghai Party Secretariat (1958) and director of the Propaganda Department of Shanghai Party branch (1963). In October 1966, Zhang became deputy head of the Cultural Revolution Group. He was elected to Politburo of the 9th Central Committee (1969) and became a member of the Standing Committee of Politburo of the 10th Central Committee (1973). In 1975, he was appointed vice-premier. In October 1976, Zhang was arrested. During the subsequent trial against the Gang of Four, Zhang did not utter one single word in his defence. He was sentenced to death with a two-year reprieve and permanent deprivation of political rights in January 1981.

Sun Dayu (1905–1997) was a celebrated translator and expert on Shakespeare studies. After graduation from Tsing Hua College in 1925, he studied at Dartmouth College (U.S.) from 1926 to 1928 and Yale University (U.S.) from 1928 to 1930. He came back to China in 1930 and became a professor, teaching in institutes that included Wuhan University, Peking Normal College, Liberal Arts College for Girls of National Peking University, Peking University, Qingdao University, Zhejiang University, Jinan University, Central School of Governance, Fudan University, and East China Normal University. He spent most of his time in prison after 1950. His works include the Chinese translation of eight plays of Shakespeare, namely *King Lear, Hamlet, Othello, Macbeth, The Merchant of Venice, The Winter's Tale, The Tempest*, and *Romeo and Juliet*, as well as writings like *Selected Poems of Qu Yuan, Selected English Poems Rendered into Chinese*, and *An Anthology of Ancient Chinese Poetry and Prose*. He also published an anthology of poetry: *Self Portrait, Goddess of Spirit and Love,* and *Collected Poems and Prose of Sun Dayu.*

Zhang Bojun (1895–1969) traveled to Germany to study philosophy at Berlin University (Humboldt-Universität zu Berlin) in 1922 and joined the Chinese Communist Party in 1923. In 1926, he returned to China and became a professor at Sun Yat-sen University. He participated in the Northern Expedition, the "August First" military uprising at Nanchang, the foundation of the Chinese Revolutionary Party, the foundation of the China Democratic League, and the Political Consultative Conference. After 1949, he served as a member of the Central People's Government Commission, councilor of the Government Administration Council, Minister of Transportation, president of the Chinese Democratic Party of Peasants and Workers, vice-president of the China Democratic League, and president of *Guangming Daily*. He was declared "China's number one Rightist" in 1957.

Chu Anping (1909–1966) graduated from Kwang Hua University in 1932 and was appointed editor of the *Central Daily* supplement. He went to the University of London (U.K.) in 1936. After returning to China in 1938, he became editor of *Central Daily*, a professor at Fudan University and the president and chief editor of the *Observer*. After 1949, he served as deputy director of the Release Management Bureau of National Press and Publication Administration, was editor-in-chief of *Guangming Daily*, and deputy chief of the Publicity Department of the Central Committee. He was criticized by Mao Zedong in 1957, then was persecuted, and went missing in 1966.

Chen Renbing (1909–1990) earned his PhD in philosophy from the University of Michigan (U.S.) in 1936. Positions he held included professor and dean of the Liberal Arts College at Shanghai St. John's University, professor in the History Department at Fudan University, and a member of the China Democratic League. In 1957, he was accused of being a Rightist. He was one of the five people who have never been rehabilitated as a Rightist.

Yan Zuyou (1943–2022), author of *Humane Comedy*, entered Shanghai Normal University in 1961, got arrested in 1964, and was rehabilitated in 1980. He had been a shop assistant, middle school teacher, and journalist before his retirement in 2003.

Xu Jian (1904–1995), author of monographs on Chinese railway engineering theories, graduated from the Civil Engineering Department at Cornell University (U.S.) in 1928 and entered Massachusetts Institute of Technology (MIT) in the same year. He did his internship with the American railway for a year after graduating before he went back to China and started teaching at Tsinghua University in 1930. He worked for Nanjing Railway Engineering Department from 1931 to 1933, Nanjing-Jiangxi Railway from 1936 to 1938, and Hunan-Guangxi Railway from 1940 to 1945. After 1949, he served as chief of the Planning Bureau of the Ministry of Railway, researcher at the Route Division of the China Academy of Railway Sciences, and was the first chief of the Architectural Studies Department at the China Academy of Railway Sciences.

Wang Shizhuo (1905–1991) earned his master's degree in aeronautical engineering from MIT in 1928, after which he stayed in the university to study engineering management. When he went back to China he became a professor in the Aviation Division in the Engineering Department at National Tsinghua University (today Tsinghua University). From 1934 to 1935, he led the design and construction of the earliest two aeronautical wind tunnels in China, located in Peking and Nanchang. In 1941, he left for the U.S. and served as the technical contact of the Aviation Department at China Defense Supplies. Inc. (CDS) and a staff member of the Representative Office of the Aviation Committee in the U.S. He then became director of the Dading Aero Engine Manufacturing Plant in 1945 and was appointed deputy director of the Aviation Industry Bureau. After the People's Republic of China was established, he was criticized and persecuted until the Cultural Revolution ended. Later, he served as a councilor of the State Council.

Qian Xuesen (1911–2009), known as the "Father of Chinese Rocketry" and the "King of Rocketry," studied at the Mechanical Engineering Department at Shanghai Chiao Tung University in 1934 and earned a Master of Science from the Aviation Engineering Department at MIT in 1936 after a year of study. From 1936 to 1939, he was a PhD candidate of the Aviation and Mathematics Department at the California Institute of Technology (U.S.) and continued to teach there after graduation. From 1946 to 1949, he was an associate professor in the Aviation and Engineering Department at MIT and later a professor of aerodynamics. From 1949 to 1955, he served as director and professor in the Jet Propulsion Laboratory at the California Institute of Technology. Positions he held after returning to China in 1955 included director at the Mechanics Institute of the Chinese Academy of Sciences, director of the Fifth Academy at the Ministry of National Defense, deputy minister of the Seventh Ministry of Machine Building, deputy director of the Commission for Science, Technology and Industry for National Defense, and vice-chairman of the Chinese People's Political Consultative Conference (CPPCC.) His works include *Engineering Cybernetics, On Systems Engineering,* and *Introduction to Interplanetary Travel.*

Gao Shiqi (1905–1988) studied at Tsing Hua College from 1918 to 1925. In 1926, he transferred from the Inorganic Chemistry Department at the University of Wisconsin to the Chemistry Department and Bacteriology Department at the University of Chicago, receiving his bachelor's degree in 1927. During his PhD studies in the Medicine School at the University of Chicago, he was permanently disabled due to viral infection in the lab. After returning to China in 1930, he served as the director of the laboratory at Nanjing University, and took up writing and translating in 1931. He was then appointed as the technical consultant of the Inter-Allied Services Department and the director of the Food Science Institute. After 1949, he served successively as a consultant for the Science Popularization Bureau in the Ministry of Culture, consultant for the All-China Association for Science Popularization, consultant for the Science Popularization Committee of the Chinese Medical Association, honorary chairman of the China Science Writing Society, and a standing councilor and consultant for the China Association for Science and Technology. He published multiple monographs on popular science.

Tang Peisong (1903–2001), one of the co-founders of modern plant physiology in China, earned his bachelor's degree in plant physiology from the University of Minnesota (U.S.) in 1927 and got a PhD in plant physiology from Johns Hopkins University (U.S.) in 1930; he then completed his postdoctoral research at Harvard University (U.S.). After going back to China he was a teacher at Wuhan University, research professor at the Research Institute for Agricultural Sciences, Tsinghua University, president of the Agriculture School at Tsinghua University, vice-president of the Beijing Agricultural University, and researcher at the Botany Institute at Chinese Academy of Sciences, where he was later promoted to deputy director, director, and honorary director. During this time, he also served as a professor and director of the teaching and research group for plant physiology at Peking University.

Hu Yaobang (1915–1989) joined the China Communist Youth League in 1930; since then, he embarked on years of political life in the Chinese Communist forces. In the autumn of 1952, he became the secretary for the Secretariat of the Central Committee of the New Democratic Youth League. After the Cultural Revolution, he was one of the main leaders responsible for re-assessing the fates of people who had been persecuted and was a promoter of reform and opening. He was elected Party Secretary General in 1980 but was forced to resign in 1987.

Chapter Eight

Tong Yin (alias Zhongshu; 1903–1977), Tong Jun's younger brother, moved with his family to Mukden (known as Shenyang today) in 1905, and studied in Fengtian First Primary School and thereafter in Nanman Secondary School. In 1925, he graduated from the Technical University of Port Arthur, after which he pursued further education in Japan and worked at the Osaka Harbor Power Station. Upon his return to China in 1928, he first worked for the Mukden Electric Light Factory and then became the chief engineer of the Cannon Factory of the Arsenal of the Three Northeastern Provinces of China. He joined the Manchurian Electric Company in Changchun in 1934 and took part in the design and construction of the Fengman Dam, which was the third-largest artificial lake at the time. In 1937, he worked on the design and planning of the Buxin Power Plant. From 1937 to 1945, he served as the chief engineer of the Harbin Electric Power Bureau and the Mukden Electric Power Bureau and held positions as acting director and director of the Northeast Electric Administration from 1945 to 1957. In 1959, he was rehabilitated from the accusation of being a Rightist, after which he worked as an ordinary engineer and a member of the China Democratic League. He died of lung cancer in 1977.

Tong Enge (1868–1945) was Tong Jun's father. He was born in the east suburb of Mukden with a Manchurian family name, Niohuru, connected to the Qing Empire. Gifted in classical Chinese, he passed through the regional, provincial, and national competitive examination for the State official selection process, and was eventually granted the final interview with the emperor and awarded with the ranking of *jinshi*. He was then assigned to the government position at Mukden, as the education director of the three northeastern Manchurian provinces and founding director of the Mukden Public Library, and the founding principal of the Mukden women's school. The Japanese sweeping into Mukden resulted in his exile. He died of a stroke in 1945.

Guan Weiran (née Suwen; 1900–1956) was born into a Bordered Yellow Banner Manchurian family in the winter of 1900 in Mukden, under the family name of Gūwalgiya. In 1919, she graduated from Shenyang First Girls' Normal College and after, married Tong Jun and changed her name to Tong Weiran. She worked as a primary school teacher in Shenyang from 1920 to 1931, during which she taught the sons of Zhang Zuolin, namely Zhang Xuesi, Zhang Xuesen, and Zhang Xuejun, as well as the famous expert on analytical instrument technology, Zhu Liangyi. After the Mukden Incident in 1931, she followed Tong Jun to Beijing in exile and arrived in Shanghai in 1932, taking care of her husband and children at home. When Shanghai fell, Tong Jun went to Chongqing while Guan Weiran stayed in Shanghai. She reunited with Tong Jun in Shanghai after the victory of the Second Sino-Japanese War and moved to Nanjing in 1947. In August 1956, she died of a heart attack, caused by a recurrence of rheumatic heart disease.

Zhang Xuesi (1916–1970) was the fourth son of Zhang Zuolin and younger brother of Zhang Xueliang. He joined the China Communist Party in 1933 and graduated from Nanjing Central Military Academy in 1937. The positions he held included president of Liaoning Provincial Government, the military commander of Liaoning Command, the vice-president of the Northeast Administrative Committee, and president of Northeastern University in Benxi. After 1949, he served as the vice-president and deputy commissar of Dalian Naval Academy and the deputy chief-of-staff of the navy. He was detained in 1967 and died in prison in 1970.

Zhang Liwu (1909–1981) graduated from Peking Normal College in 1935, and later served as the chief editor of *New Shandong Culture and New Shandong Newspaper*, and the president of Shandong University, the vice-president of Shenyang Institute of Technology, the vice-president of the Northeast Institute of Technology, and vice-president of Liaoning University. He was accused of being a Rightist in 1957.

En Yuzhi, wife of Tong Yin (younger brother of Tong Jun), died from starvation and disease while Tong Yin was held in custody.

Zhao Ruilin, wife of Tong Cun (youngest brother of Tong Jun), suffered a mental breakdown when Tong Cun was persecuted during the Cultural Revolution.

Chapter Nine

Deng Siling (1931–) is a professor at Southeast University.

Pan Guxi (1928–), chief editor of *History of Chinese Architecture*, studied at the Architecture Departments at National Central University and Nanjing University from 1947 to 1951. He took up teaching after graduation and took part in the writing of *Classical Gardens of Suzhou*, led by Liu Dunzhen.

Zhu Guangfeng was a student from the Department of Architecture at Nanjing Institute of Technology who took Tong Jun's medals and other properties in a house raid during the Cultural Revolution.

Wang Caizhong was an activist who denunciated and persecuted professors during the Cultural Revolution. He later expressed his regret to some of the professors he had beaten.

Chapter Ten

Gu Danyun (1941–2022), wife of Tong Linbi (the third son of Tong Jun), was among China's first generation of aerospace scientists. From 1960 to 1965, she served as a second lieutenant in the third detachment of No. 743 Army of Chinese PLA. She dedicated her life to China's aerospace industry, participating in projects like Dongfeng ballistic missiles, Hongqi series missiles, wind radar, and electron-positron collider.

Qian Sanqiang (1913–1992), founder of the Chinese nuclear industry, graduated from Tsinghua University in 1936, then went to France in 1937 to undertake research under the Curies; he attained his PhD in 1940 from University of Paris (France). In 1946, he received the Henri de Parville Award for Physics from the French Academy of Sciences. He worked as a researcher at the French National Centre for Scientific Research in 1947 before returning to China to take up a professorial position in the Physics Department at Tsinghua University in 1948. In 1951, he served as the director of the Modern Physics Institute at the Chinese Academy of Sciences and was appointed as vice-minister of the Third Ministry of Machine Building. During the Cultural Revolution, he was denounced as a reactionary academic authority. In 1978, he became vice-president of the Chinese Academy of Sciences while concurrently serving as the president of Zhejiang University.

Xiao Qingyun (Ching-Yuen Hsiao; 1900–1984) graduated from Tsing Hua College in 1924 and earned his bachelor's in civil engineering from the California Institute of Technology (U.S.) in 1926, and master's and PhD from Harvard University (U.S.) in 1927 and 1930 respectively. Upon his return to China, he worked for the Shanghai municipal government, and later with the Ministry of Communications of the Republic of China. In 1946, he was awarded the Medal of Freedom by President Truman for his meritorious contribution in the war against Japan. From 1947 to 1957, he served as the delegate for China on the United Nations Transportation and Communication Commission. He settled in the United States 1949, and since then served as the Chinese Director of the Ministry of Transportation until he retired in 1969, after which he provided service for churches and parks.

Zhan Hongying (1935–) is the wife of Tong Jun's second son, Tong Linsu, the emeritus professor of the Southeast University. She graduated from the Power Electronics and Nuclear Energy Department at Nanjing

Institute of Technology in 1959. From 1960 to 2003, she taught in the Department of Radio Engineering (now School of Information Science and Engineering at Southeast University), specializing the research on the sensors, data convertors, and precision measurement technologies.

Chapter Eleven

Zhu Qiqian (1872–1964) served as the Minister of Transportation for five terms and the Minister of Internal Affairs for three terms for the Beiyang Government. He was also the chief of the Preparatory Office for the Emperor Proclamation Ceremony for Yuan Shikai and the acting prime minister of the Beiyang Government. He founded the first public park, Central Park in Beijing, the first Cultural Heritage Exhibition Hall in China, and the Society for Research in Chinese Architecture (SRCA).

Li Jie (1035–1110) served as the chief of the Construction Supervision Office in 1092, overseeing the construction of palaces, city walls, bridges, mansions, houses, and roads. He led the construction of the Mansion for Five Princes, Zhuque Gate, Jinglong Gate, Jiucheng Palace, Imperial Ancestral Temple, Empress Dowager Qinci Buddhist Temple, and Imperial Academy, as well as the Department of State Affairs, Government Office of Kaifeng, and Barracks for Imperial Guards. In 1100, he completed the book *Yingzao Fashi (Song Manual Building Standards)*, which is the most important monograph on architecture in ancient China; the book was published in 1103.

Mo Zongjiang (Tsung-chiang Mo; 1916–1999) joined the Society for Research in Chinese Architecture in 1931, serving as a draftsman, and later a student researcher and an associate researcher, helping Liang Sicheng with his studies. In 1946, he joined the Department of Architecture at Tsinghua University, working as a lecturer, associate professor, and professor. His written articles include "The Yuhua Palace of the Yongshou Temple," "The White Pagoda Tomb of Jiuzhou Dam, Yibin from the Song Dynasty,""The Wenshu Palace of the Geyuan Temple in Laiyuan," and "Styles and Techniques of the Sculptures in the Cave Temple of Gongxian," in collaboration with Chen Mingda.

— INDEX —

Page references in **bold** refer to images.

F

Fairbank, John King 93–95
Fairbank, Wilma 23, 57–58, 85, 93–95, 100, 106, 215
Fan Wenzhao 67, 193, 227
Fang Yong 21, 27, 28, 30, 37–39, 73, 214

G

Gao Shiqi 117–19, 238–39, **120**
Glimpses of Gardens in Eastern China, see *Dongnan Yuanshu*
Gu Danyun 156, 242
Guan Songsheng 68, 226, 227–28
Guan Weiran 103, 126, 127, 143, 155–56, 206, 240, 247, **154, 157, 172**
Guo Husheng 25, 28, 188, 216
Guo Yuanxi 57, 224
Guo Yulin 99, 231

H

Ha Xiongwen 57, 224
Hu Shi 53, 191, 220
Hu Yaobang 119, 198, 239
Huang Jiahua 57, 223
Huang Xueshi 57, 225
Huang Yiluan 43, 146, 217

J

Jiang Jieshi, *see* Chiang Kai-shek
Jiangnan Yuanlin Zhi 43–44, 46, 53–54, 109, 121, 153, 171–84, 208, 210, **177**

L

Li Gongpu 111, 234
Li Jie 173, 203, 243
Liang Qichao 53, 71–72, 96, 100, 191, 218
Liang Shiqiu 56, 222
Liang Sicheng 9–11, 16, 23, 57, 58, 60, 67, 71–72, 74, 93–98, 100–102, 104, 129, 172–73, 176, 176, 187, 215–16, **97, 99, 105, 106, 177**
Liang Yan 57, 224–25
Lin Huiyin 67, 71, 93–95, 100–101, 102, 104, 174, 193, 227
Lin Tongji 57, 81–82, 119–21, 223–24
Lin Zhu 58–60, 226

Liu Dunzhen 12, 14, 15, 16, 106, 136, 172–74, 175, 178–79, 181–82, 190, 217–18, 229, 241

Liu Guanghua 72–73, 146–47, 194, 216, **138**
Liu Hongdian 99, 230–31
Liu Xujie 181–82
Liu Zhiping 99, 173, 231–32
Luo Longji 111, 116, 233

M

Ma, John 53, 220
Marco Polo Bridge Incident 174–75, 176
Mei Yiqi 53, 219–20
Mo Zongjiang 174, 243

N

Nanjing Institute of Technology 39–40, 73, 82, 88, 98, 103, 137, 143–44, 147, 156, **38**, see also Central University, Southeast University
Northeastern University (Northeast Technical College) 71–72, 88, 96, 98–103, 127–31

O

On Classical Gardens in Southeastern China, see Jiangnan Yuanlin Zhi

P

Pan Guxi 142, 241
Peng Wenying 111, 112, 116, 233

Q

Qi Kang 24, 26, 142, 143, 216
Qian Sanqiang 156, 242
Qian Xuesen 117, 238

S

September 18 Incident 98, 103
Sha Qianli 111, 234–35
Shao Yu 82, 230
Shen Junru 111, 234
Shi Liang 111, 112, 235
Song Qingling 112, 235
Southeast University 46, 90, see also Central University, Nanjing Institute of Technology

writing 11, 14–15, 24, 43–48, 109, 119, 162, 164–65, 172–82, 211, *see also individual works*

youth 8–9

Tong Lang 222

Tong Linbi 57, 103, 158, 215

Tong Linsu 30, 40, 47, 65, 66, 75–76, 104, 115, 119, 132, 142, 143, 153, 156, 217, **154**

Tong Ming 90, 109, 141, 148, 183, **110**

Tong Shibai 57, 58, 60, 98–99, 155, 171–72, 220–21, **56**, **59**, **154**, **172**

Tong Wei 30–32, 60, 126, 217, **56**

Tong Wen 21, 23, 24, 25, 27, 40, 43, 44, 46, 47, 53, 56, 74, 86, 96, 109, 121, 126, 132, 142, 143, 147, 148, 155, 156, 158–62, 163–66, 178, 183, 214, **110**, **160**

Tong Yan 86, 230

Tong Yin 9, 125–26, 129, 131, 132–34, 158, 239, **133**, **134**

Tsinghua University (Tsing Hua College) 51–53, 58, 60, 71, 74, 93, 101, 104, 219–21, 223, 226, 230, 232, 237, 239, 242, 243

W

Wang Caizhong 144, 241

Wang Guowei 5, 53–54, 179–80, 218

Wang Huabin 57, 225

Wang Shizhuo 117–19, 237–38, **118**, **120**

Wang Shu 45–46, 87, 180, 190, 217

Wang Tingfang 29–30, 188, 217

Wang Wenxian 53, 219

Wang Zaoshi 111, 233

Wen Yiduo 56, 221

Wen Yiqi 56, 222

Wu Liangyong 58, 86, 87, 192, 226, **59**, **84**

X

Xiang Bingren 21, 25–28, 214

Xiao Qingyun 162, 242

Xu Jian 117, 237, **120**, **121**

Y

Yan Longyu 24, 28, 37, 216

Yan Zuyou 116, 237

Published in Australia in 2024 by
The Images Publishing Group Pty Ltd
ABN 89 059 734 431

Offices

Melbourne
Waterman Business Centre
Suite 64, Level 2 UL40
1341 Dandenong Road
Chadstone, Victoria 3148
Australia
Tel: +61 3 8564 8122

New York
6 West 18th Street 4B
New York City, NY 10011
United States
Tel: +1 212 645 1111

Shanghai
6F, Building C,
838 Guangji Road
Hongkou District,
Shanghai 200434
China
Tel: +86 021 31260822

books@imagespublishing.com
www.imagespublishing.com

 A catalogue record for this
book is available from the
National Library of Australia

Title: A Solitary Traveler in the Long Night: Tong Jun—The Later Years 1963–1983
Author: Zhang Qin (Translated by Howard Goldblatt)
ISBN: 9781864709438

IMAGES has included on its website a page for special notices in relation to this and its other
publications. Please visit www.imagespublishing.com

Every effort has been made to trace the original source of copyright material contained in this book.
The publishers would be pleased to hear from copyright holders to rectify any errors or omissions.

The information and illustrations in this publication have been prepared and supplied by Zhang Qin,
Howard Goldblatt, and Tom Ming. While all reasonable efforts have been made to ensure accuracy,
the publishers do not, under any circumstances, accept responsibility for errors, omissions and
representations express or implied.

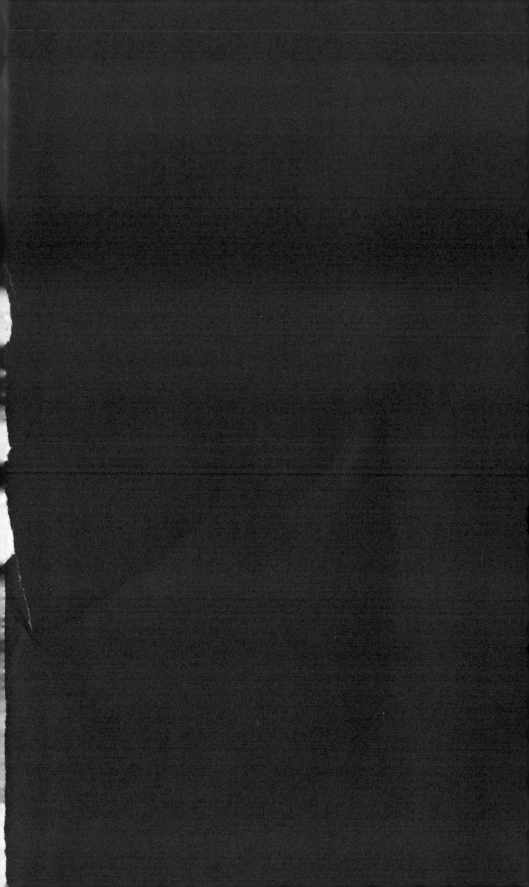